Advance Praise

"From design missteps to billion-dollar turnarounds, this book is a master class in navigating the high-risk world of packaging design change."

—JENNIFER PICARD, GLOBAL INSIGHTS
TRANSFORMATION LEAD, OPELLA

"Behaviorally's 4S framework gave our teams a shared language and the clarity to make fast, confident decisions."

—KEN HAUSER, SENIOR MANAGER MARKET
RESEARCH, CHURCH AND DWIGHT CO., INC.

"This book dives into case studies and key packaging design principles every marketer should know."

—JON ZUNICK, INNOVATION MANAGER, BAYER

"This book isn't about tools—it's about changing how we make decisions."

—JOHN D. PFALZGRAF, DIRECTOR, CONSUMER
KNOWLEDGE, GEORGIA-PACIFIC

"This book is a must-read for any marketer serious about converting packaging into a revenue driver. The data doesn't lie—visibility alone can 2.5x your likelihood of purchase."

—SARA POLON, CO-FOUNDER AND CEO, SOUPERGIRL

"This book brilliantly captures what marketers have felt for years— packaging is your first, best salesperson."

—NINO CIAPPINA, GENERAL MANAGER, AUTOMOTIVE, WALMART MARKETPLACE

"Every CPG executive should read unPACKED. It's a powerful reminder that packaging isn't just a design tool; it's one of your most overlooked and impactful growth levers."

—NICK GRAHAM, FOUNDER, VERTEMIS

"This book is a must-have toolkit to understand value creation through packaging in a fast-changing consumer omni-channel shopping environment."

—FRANCESCO VENTISETTE, EXECUTIVE DIRECTOR, INSIGHT AND ANALYTICS, BAUSCH + LOMB

unPACKED.

unPACKED.

Predict Packaging That Sells

Alex Hunt and Matt Salem

LIONCREST
PUBLISHING

unPACKED

Predict Packaging That Sells

FIRST EDITION

ISBN   978-1-5445-4941-5 *Hardcover*

978-1-5445-4940-8 *Paperback*

978-1-5445-4942-2 *Ebook*

978-1-5445-4943-9 *Audiobook*

To anyone who has ever reimagined the predictive power of consumer insights, trading gut feel for evidence and precision. This book is for you.

CONTENTS

FOREWORD

—Bianca Pryor, AI & Insights Professional

The insights industry has always been in need of innovation. No, disruption. For decades, we have consistently worked to understand what shoppers and consumers want to influence behavior and ultimately, most importantly, drive sales. And in today's fragmented world, the stakes are insanely high. Stopping power and navigation cues are no longer enough.

That's what makes *unPACKED* such a timely and essential read. Alex Hunt and Matt Salem have captured a transformation in the making. Drawing on decades of behavioral research and data-driven experience, they reveal how packaging design decisions can now be made with the speed, precision, and confidence today's brands demand. This isn't theory. It's not a list of best practices or a retrospective on good design. This is the future: packaging decisions powered by predictive insight, made in real time, and grounded in how people actually shop.

What sets this book apart is its clarity. It translates complex ideas into practical strategies without losing their depth. It's packed with case studies, human stories, and market realities that anyone in our field will recognize immediately, from missed redesign opportunities to breakthrough successes. It's a handbook for navigating real-world challenges, with tools built for researchers, marketers, brand managers, and creative teams who want to get packaging right the first time.

unPACKED invites us to embrace better data and challenges us to rethink the very role of packaging research in brand building. As someone who has spent a career helping brands succeed and always pushing insights to add greater commercial value, I can confidently say this: If you care about driving results, this book belongs on your desk. Not someday—now.

Read it. Share it. Use it.

Because in our line of work, the margin between being seen and being forgotten is thinner than ever.

INTRODUCTION

Packaging drives sales. But it's harder than it looks.

In today's fragmented retail landscape, a great product isn't enough. Whether you're a global brand or a startup on shelf for the first time, your packaging has to do more—and do it faster. Your packaging must be seen, understood, trusted, and chosen. And it must achieve all of that in the blink of an eye, across physical aisles and digital thumbnails, for shoppers with infinite options and shifting expectations. Research methods and insights capabilities haven't kept up with this pace. This book showcases the disruptions that do that.

We believe packaging can become a source of strategic clarity. One that unites creative teams, insight professionals, and decision-makers around a common goal: to win at shelf. By productizing behavioral science, pairing it with our best-in-class database, and connecting it to sales data through predictive AI, we can finally align behind what truly drives purchase behavior. We can move faster, test smarter, and predict performance with unprecedented accuracy.

If you're a brand leader, insights professional, designer, or CMO tasked with launching or evolving consumer goods, this book is for you. You'll learn how to navigate real-world packaging challenges, leverage data in new ways, and build internal alignment around designs that are not only creative but commercially successful. Here's what this book is:

- A practical, story-driven guide to the future of packaging research
- A behind-the-scenes look at how leading brands are using behavioral diagnostics and predictive products to make better commercial decisions
- A handbook for faster, smarter, more collaborative packaging processes, each equally applicable to adjacent elements of the marketing mix

Here's what it isn't:

- A theoretical exploration of design thinking
- A dense academic treatise on AI or behavioral science
- A rigid methodology manual with a single way forward

We wrote this book because we've seen firsthand how much is at stake and how much potential is being left on the table. We've sat in the meetings, navigated the silos, and helped teams align around the packaging that performs. And now with the right products, the right data, and the right mindset, we believe it's possible to make those high-stakes decisions with confidence and precision.

In the chapters that follow, you'll explore how our predictive packaging engine works and how we've transformed decades of behavioral data into productized tools that help brands make faster, smarter, and more profitable packaging decisions. We'll share real case studies from Behaviorally's clients, firsthand stories from the field, and insights drawn from the challenges brands face every day at shelf.

This is not just a book about methodology. It's a window into a new era of packaging research that delivers measurable commercial impact.

We believe the future of packaging research is predictive, dynamic, and deeply human. And we believe the time to embrace that future is now. In these pages you'll find not only a vision of what's possible, but a practical guide to the products, strategies, and mindsets that are already reshaping the way packaging decisions are made.

Let's turn the page and reimagine what packaging research can do.

Chapter 1.

PACKAGING IS MISSION CRITICAL

Walk down any chocolate aisle around the globe, and you'll see a rainbow of wrappers: some elegant, some nostalgic, some trying very, very hard to be edgy. But which packs actually work? Which packs get picked up, carried to the checkout, and converted into a purchase?

To find out, we rolled up our sleeves and analyzed the data. Our *unPACKED: Chocolates Report* took a deep dive into more than 300 chocolate SKUs in the US including established names, upstarts, and everything in between and measured how well each one performed across key behavioral metrics:

- How visible it is on shelf
- How shoppable it feels
- How desirable it seems
- Whether it ultimately makes the short list for purchase

Grounded in a behavioral study conducted by our team in August 2024, we analyzed the actions of roughly 3,000 chocolate shoppers across the US[1], and the findings were clear: Being seen is everything.

In the chocolate category, products that were most visible on shelf were more than 2.5x more likely to be purchased than those that weren't.[2] That number jumps even higher when you isolate the top-performing SKUs. Visibility drives sales. Period.

But visibility alone isn't enough.

Some packs were eye-catching but failed to communicate clearly. Others were seen but were difficult to find. And some blended into the background, losing opportunity for consideration in the first place.

We saw firsthand how shelf position, design contrast, brand blocking, and adjacent categories shape how chocolate is perceived and ultimately chosen. And we tracked the real behavioral impact of design decisions.

This is the power of unPACKED, our human-led, data-backed look at what drives performance in today's most competitive categories. Chocolate is just one example.

TONY'S CHOCOLONELY: CHOCOLATE'S BREAKOUT STAR

As of 2023, chocolate is a $119.39 billion industry. By 2032, it's projected to grow to $161.99 billion,[3] but it's overwhelmingly controlled by a small handful of major brands, with the majority of sales coming from just 10 companies.[4] That leaves hundreds of smaller brands fighting over what remains, making it incredibly difficult for new players to gain meaningful traction.

Tony's Chocolonely entered this ultra-competitive space with a mission-driven product: a premium chocolate brand dedicated to fighting child labor and unfair trade practices in the cocoa industry.[5] But having a mission wasn't enough; they needed a way to cut through the noise, capture attention, and convince shoppers to switch from established brands.

With packaging that breaks all the rules, Tony's Chocolonely stands out in the chocolate aisle, and that's exactly the point. While most chocolate brands utilize deep browns, golds, and elegant designs, Tony's goes bold with bright, eye-popping colors that practically jump off the shelf. The vibrant, clashing hues make it impossible to ignore, creating a visual explosion that grabs your attention instantly.

The brand name itself is big, loud, and deliberately chunky with irregular typography. It's slightly off-kilter, reinforcing Tony's rebellious, rule-breaking personality. This isn't just another polished, refined chocolate bar; it's a statement piece, loud and proud.

Tony's continues to defy the rules with an unconventional layout. Unlike the minimalist style of most premium chocolates, its packaging feels playful, imperfect, and unapologetically different. It's fun, vibrant, and full of personality, making it easy to spot and even easier to remember.

But Tony's doesn't stop at eye-catching design; it uses every element of its packaging to tell a story. Inside, the chocolate itself is divided into unequal pieces, a deliberate choice symbolizing the inequality in the cocoa industry. It's a powerful design decision that reinforces Tony's social impact mission, reminding consumers that their purchase supports the fight for fair trade and ethical sourcing.

Tony's Chocolonely proves that packaging can be more than just a wrapper. It can be a movement.

The results are undeniable. Tony's Chocolonely quickly became the fastest-growing chocolate brand in the US and UK capturing over $200.1 million in revenue in 2023/2024.[6]

By using packaging as a marketing tool, Tony's Chocolonely turned an unknown brand into a sensation. One that stood out visually, ethically, and emotionally.

THE EMOTIONAL PULL OF PACKAGING

Take it from Tony Chocolonely: Successful packaging is about function and visibility.

But did you know that packaging is also a powerful tool for creating emotional connections? Brands work hard to create emotional ties with shoppers, so they can be selected at shelf *and* build loyalty with their customer. Packaging plays a critical role in reinforcing those feelings.

One way to see this in action is by drawing a comparison to advertising. Think about a heartfelt commercial like the ones featuring babies, families, or moments of joy. Those ads are effective because they tap into universal emotions, making consumers feel something about the brand. Packaging operates in the same way, just in a more immediate and visual form, often in the moment of purchase.

Let's look at diaper brands for example. It isn't easy to find a pack of diapers that doesn't feature a baby. The image isn't just decorative; it taps into the emotions of parents, reinforcing the instinct to nurture and protect. Even some brands that *aren't* baby-related use this strategy. Angel Soft toilet paper has long featured a baby on its packaging, leveraging that same emotional cue, but in this case to signal softness and comfort.

The same principle applies to food. A rich, indulgent visual of melted chocolate or a sizzling burger isn't solely about showing the product; it's about triggering desire. Appetite appeal is a direct emotional driver. It makes shoppers crave the product before they pick it up even if the burger in the packaging is still frozen.

Some brands use emotion more subtly. Claritin's packaging, with its bright blue sky and green fields, doesn't scream "allergy relief" in a literal sense, but it does create an emotional connection to freedom, relaxation, and being outdoors without discomfort. Instead of focusing purely on clinical benefits, it sells a feeling, one that resonates deeply with allergy sufferers looking for an escape from their symptoms.

There are scientific and psychological reasons why certain packaging elements stick in consumers' minds. In this chapter, you'll discover why packaging matters not as a protective container, but as one of the most powerful tools a brand has to influence perception and drive growth. You'll learn how packaging works as a silent salesperson on the shelf, sparking emotional connections, reinforcing brand identity, and guiding consumers through the purchase journey. Through real-world examples, we'll show how packaging can elevate a product, create market differentiation, and even launch entire brands. Whether you're refining an established icon or trying to break into a crowded category, this chapter reveals why packaging isn't part of the product delivery alone; it is part of the product experience.

JACK DANIEL'S: ELEVATING A PREMIUM VARIANT

Gentleman Jack
Before

Gentleman Jack
After

Jack Daniel's

Jack Daniel's is one of the most iconic whiskey brands in the world, best known for its signature Old No. 7 bottle. But within its portfolio sits Gentleman Jack, a smoother, double-mellowed variant aimed at premium whiskey drinkers. While Gentleman Jack had some initial success, its original packaging closely resembled Old No. 7, using a square bottle structure and a black label. The issue? It didn't visually distinguish itself enough from the parent product, making differentiated and premium perception harder to command.

Jack Daniel's needed a packaging overhaul that would reinforce Gentleman Jack's premium positioning, and it delivered in a way that led to a staggering 40% increase in sales.[7]

The new Gentleman Jack packaging departed entirely from the traditional Jack Daniel's bottle shape. The initial redesign changes weren't subtle. They were strategic and bold, designed to elevate the brand's premium feel:

- A taller, more elongated structure: Moving away from the boxy Old No. 7 shape, the new bottle featured a sleeker, refined silhouette, instantly signaling a more premium offering.
- Metallic branding elements: The redesign incorporated metallic labels and accents, a proven tactic in the alcoholic beverage category that reinforces luxury and exclusivity.
- A premium cap and embossed details: These subtle but impactful touches created a stronger tactile experience, making the bottle feel as premium as the whiskey inside.
- Enhanced signature branding: Gentleman Jack's branding became more distinct, featuring elegant typography and embossed lettering that elevated its visual appeal.

The results of the redesign were undeniable: Sales shot up 40%, a rare and remarkable achievement in the ultra-competitive whiskey market.

This success speaks to a fundamental truth about premium

product packaging: Perception drives value. Consumers weren't just buying whiskey; they were buying the experience, and packaging played a crucial role in reinforcing that.

Jack Daniel's didn't change the whiskey inside the bottle; it changed how consumers perceived it.

The Gentleman Jack redesign is a prime example of how structure, material choices, and visual elements can come together to elevate a product's value perception without altering the product itself. By aligning the packaging with consumer expectations of a premium whiskey, Jack Daniel's successfully:

- Strengthened differentiation from its core product (Old No. 7)
- Increased perceived quality and value through metallics, structure, and branding cues
- Justified a higher price point and encouraged new consumers to trade up

Gentleman Jack's transformation proves that in premium categories, packaging isn't just a container; it's part of the product experience itself. And when executed well, it doesn't only elevate perception, but also directly drives sales.

WHY PACKAGING MATTERS

Packaging matters because it drives sales.

To understand why, we have to take a step back and look at the broader landscape of consumer packaged goods (CPG).

In 2024, the global CPG market was valued at $2.299 trillion annually and is projected to grow to $3.436 trillion by 2034.[8]

Beyond topline revenue, the CPG sector plays a pivotal role in the broader US economy. It contributes $2.5 trillion in total economic impact (nearly 10%) and supports more than 22.3 million American jobs.[9] This impact is magnified by the sale of consumer goods in almost every market around the world.

This large industry is characterized by steady growth and tight margins. For years, global branding helped expand profitability, but today's consumers are more demanding, requesting more personalized experiences, and forcing brands to rethink how they engage and sell. For a CEO, growth is always top priority and is now harder to achieve than ever. Post-COVID-19, companies took advantage of pricing power and margin expansion when they could, but sustained growth remains a constant challenge. Many major CPG brands have faced disruption from activist investors, exposing just how tough it is to maintain momentum in this space. This is where packaging comes in. Unlike retail channels or product sizing, both of which involve trade-offs, design is one of the few levers brands fully control. Our studies show it can drive growth by as much as 5% (and poor packaging can *drop* sales by 5%), making it an essential, yet often underutilized, growth channel.

Beyond growth, packaging is also a major financial factor in a company's bottom line. It accounts for a significant portion of direct costs, estimated at around 8% (the industry-accepted average), which means any misstep is expensive. (Tropicana is a prime example: sales dropped 20% when it replaced its iconic packaging, resulting in an estimated $30 million loss.) A packaging change isn't just a simple swap; it can require factory reconfigurations, new sourcing agreements, and supply chain adjustments. Getting it right is absolutely critical.

THE FACE OF THE BRAND

Packaging is more than just a protective layer. It's the face of the brand, the first impression that shapes consumer perception. Just as we read facial expressions to understand someone's mood or intentions, consumers read packaging to gauge a brand's identity. There's an energy behind it, a vibe that instantly communicates what the brand is all about. It's the way a brand dresses itself, influencing how we feel about it before we even engage with the product.

Think of packaging like attire; just as clothing sets expectations about a person, packaging sets expectations for a brand. If we showed up to an interview in a crisp suit, you'd have a different impression of us than if we showed up in gym gear. It's not just about the clothes themselves; it's about the context they create. The same goes for packaging. It gives shape to the brand, providing a tangible, touchable form that communicates quality, purpose, and identity.

It's also a powerful communication tool. Packaging sets expectations. It tells consumers what the product is, who it's for, and how it fits into their lives. It's the cover of the brand's book, and we all know how quickly people judge a book by its cover. Care needs to be taken so the first impression is not misleading, as this can make or break a sale. In a competitive market, the product with the more appealing package often has a leg up, even if the content inside is identical.

THE EXPERIENCE WITH THE BRAND

This perception-shaping power is so influential that packaging alone can change how consumers experience the product.

In a series of global taste and quality tests, bottled water brands including higher-end brands like Fiji didn't just underperform but lost to tap water. Fiji's water ranked lower in taste, and its overall quality was lower, too.[10]

And before you assume that's a fluke, these tests were run across multiple regions with a variety of participants. Sometimes the bottled water edged ahead in quality but not always.

So why do we keep buying it? Packaging. That sleek, see-through bottle. The hibiscus-flower imagery. The curated typography and cool-toned color palette. It's all designed to whisper "pure" and "premium" into your subconscious. Packaging shapes perception, sometimes more powerfully than the product itself does. When done well, packaging doesn't just dress up a product; it elevates, reframes, and convinces us a product is worth the price. Even when it's just water.

It's the same principle as eating with your eyes. If you're served a beautifully plated dish versus a sloppy one, even if the ingredients are identical, your perception of taste and quality will be different. Packaging is the visual experience that sets the stage for the product itself. It creates the context, the anticipation, and ultimately the satisfaction of the purchase.

This is why packaging is so critical: It communicates the brand's story, establishes expectations, and shapes consumer experiences, all within a single glance. And in today's crowded marketplace, that first impression can make all the difference.

At its core, packaging decisions aren't only about aesthetics or marketing. They are high-stakes, mission-critical choices that impact everything from sales and market share to operational efficiency and financial performance.

HEINZ 57: REINVENTING A CLASSIC WITHOUT LOSING IDENTITY

Few brands have packaging as instantly recognizable as Heinz Ketchup. The classic glass bottle, the "57 Varieties" label, and even the ritual of tapping the "57" to get the ketchup flowing have all become ingrained in consumer culture.

But as consumer habits changed, Heinz faced a challenge: The glass bottle, while iconic, wasn't always convenient. People struggled to get the ketchup out, often resorting to shaking, banging, or using knives. The functional limitations of the original bottle opened the door for innovation, but Heinz had to be careful. How do you modernize a classic without losing what makes it iconic?

Heinz executed a multistage evolution of its packaging that preserved its brand equity while significantly improving functionality.

THE GLASS BOTTLE AND THE RITUAL OF THE "57"

The iconic "57 varieties" slogan on Heinz products was never meant to reflect the actual number of items the company offered.

When founder Henry J. Heinz introduced the phrase in 1896, the brand already had over 60 products; he picked the number 57 purely for its marketing charm (5 was his lucky number, 7 was his wife's, and he believed the number 7 held universal psychological appeal).[11] Despite its inaccuracy, the number stuck and has become a core part of Heinz's brand identity ever since.

It also isn't just a branding element. The "57" embossing on the neck on the glass bottle proved to be functional, too. Consumers are instructed to tap the "57" to release the ketchup, a trick that has become part of the brand's cultural identity.[12]

This design choice blended brand recognition with user experience, reinforcing that Heinz wasn't just selling ketchup; it was selling a time-honored way to enjoy it.

THE UPSIDE-DOWN SQUEEZE BOTTLE

As consumer demand for convenience grew, Heinz introduced an upside-down plastic squeeze bottle, a major departure from its traditional glass design. To maintain its brand identity, Heinz flipped the label so that even when stored cap-down (for easy dispensing), the branding remained right side up.

This simple but intentional design choice ensured that even with a structural change, the Heinz brand remained front and center.

A NEW ICON IS BORN

Over time, the upside-down squeeze bottle became as iconic as the glass version. Packaging innovation, when executed well, can become part of a brand's legacy rather than replacing it.

The old glass bottle is now a nostalgic symbol, often found in classic diners and restaurants, while the squeeze bottle has become the everyday staple in homes. The squeeze bottle quickly became the preferred format, especially for home use, reducing complaints about ketchup being difficult to dispense.[13]

The packaging shift also led to increased brand loyalty, as Heinz successfully made the switch to convenience without sacrificing its heritage, an accomplishment in the CPG industry.

Heinz 57 is an example of a brand that successfully straddled 2 worlds: maintaining the nostalgia and cultural cachet of its original design while embracing modern functionality to stay relevant.

- The glass bottle represents brand heritage and tradition.
- The upside-down squeeze bottle represents convenience and modern usability.
- Both designs remain instantly recognizable as Heinz.

The key lesson? Iconic packaging can evolve without losing its essence. By respecting what made the original design special while addressing real consumer needs, Heinz didn't just modernize its product; it expanded its legacy.[14]

PACKAGING DRIVES SALES

A well-designed visual doesn't just catch the eye. It also emotionally connects and guides the shopper through the decision process. Every element should work together seamlessly, confirming that this is the right product, the right flavor, the right scent, and the right size. If a shopper has to hunt for key information or feels like the design is jumping from one place to another without a clear flow, the packaging isn't doing its job.

When done right, label architecture tells a story, creating a natural and intuitive experience. The shopper's eyes move effortlessly across brand name, visual cues, and key benefits to seal the deal. It's not just about looking good; it's about making the buying decision easy, fast, and instinctive.

Because at the end of the day, packaging isn't *just* a product's outfit but a tool that elicits behavior and persuasion.

Packaging persuades and drives sales in 3 powerful ways:

1. Reinforces brand loyalty
2. Attracts new customers
3. Guides shoppers through the purchase funnel

All play a crucial role in influencing consumer behavior and ultimately driving purchases.

REINFORCES BRAND LOYALTY

Packaging reassures loyal customers that they're making the right choice. It's about familiarity and consistency. When you walk down the aisle looking for a brand you know and love, the packaging needs to be exactly what you expect. Changes big or small can cause hesitation, leading to a moment of doubt.

We've all experienced it: reaching for a familiar product only to pause because something looks slightly off. That moment of uncertainty can be the difference between a purchase and walking away.

This is why consistency is so critical. Packaging should seamlessly carry consumers through their habitual buying process. When executed well, big or small changes can reinforce trust and loyalty, ensuring repeat purchases without interruption. Consistency keeps customers engaged and coming back for more by delivering the same promise they've come to expect every time they interact with the product.

ATTRACTS NEW CUSTOMERS

On the other end of the spectrum, packaging is also a powerful tool for attracting new customers. It serves as an invitation to try something new, appealing to consumers' innate curiosity and desire for new experiences. Whether it's a bold color, an innovative structural design, or an intriguing message, packaging can lure shoppers in even if they've never seen or heard of the product.

In fact, packaging can function independently of other marketing channels. It can capture attention, spark interest, and convert a browser into a buyer all on its own. It's the silent salesperson on the shelf, speaking directly to consumers and persuading them to give the product a try. Especially in CPG categories where people are more willing to experiment, effective packaging can drive trial and expand a brand's customer base.

GUIDES CONSUMERS THROUGH THE PURCHASE FUNNEL

Packaging drives sales by reinforcing brand messaging and guiding consumers (new and old) through the purchase funnel. It connects the dots between various touchpoints, creating a cohesive brand experience.

Imagine seeing a memorable ad, whether in person, on TV, or online, and then spotting the product in-store with packaging that perfectly aligns with the campaign's visuals and messaging. That moment of recognition helps complete the sale. It's the bridge between awareness and purchase, linking all elements of the marketing mix into one unified experience.

Packaging doesn't just influence the point of sale. It enhances the entire customer journey. It reinforces campaign messages, builds brand equity, and creates a seamless transition from marketing to purchase, ensuring that consumers feel confident and excited about their choice.

A HIGH-STAKES REDESIGN: MATT'S STORY

In 2010, a major beer brand underwent a significant redesign that changed the face of its iconic brand, moving from short and stout packaging to sleek and thin packaging. This was no ordinary packaging refresh. This was a seismic shift that would redefine the brand's global identity. And behind the scenes, our team was at the heart of it all, leading the packaging research and testing that would make or break this transformation.

We lovingly code-named the project "Monster," and it lived up to its name. It was colossal not only in scope but in impact. This project wasn't just about testing a few new designs; it was about evaluating every possible iteration for the company's bottles and cans and even for the secondary packaging (the 6-pack holders and cardboard carriers). This initiative aimed to modernize the brand's image and enhance its appeal to contemporary consumers.

It was a major change.

Key features of the redesign included:

- Pressure-Sensitive Label (PSL): Transitioning from glue-applied labels, the brand adopted pressure-sensitive labels for its bottles. This change allowed for a cleaner, more premium appearance and facilitated easier recycling processes.
- Bottle Shape and Design: The new bottle featured a taller, slimmer neck and stronger shoulders, giving it a more modern silhouette. An embossed name and a strategically placed thumb groove were added to improve grip and maintain the beer's cold temperature longer.
- Unified Global Identity: The redesign was implemented across all 170 markets where the brand is sold, ensuring a consistent and recognizable brand image worldwide.

This comprehensive overhaul extended beyond the primary bottle to include cans and secondary packaging elements like 6-packs and even draft kegs, all featuring updated graphics to reinforce the brand's upscale positioning. While not the most recent change, this 2013 redesign laid the groundwork for subsequent packaging innovations by establishing a cohesive and modern brand aesthetic.

The company's short-neck bottle was an icon, linked to the brand's identity. Changing that shape wasn't just about aesthetics; it was about challenging decades of brand association and consumer loyalty. We knew we had to get this right, no matter what.

As always, there was no room for error. Every detail mattered. We combed through mountains of data, double-checking every insight and making sure our recommendations were airtight. We needed to give the brand the confidence to make the right decision.

The brand team followed our recommendations, and the impact was undeniable. The new design went to market and brought global consistency to the company's look, reinforcing its brand equity while modernizing its appearance. The long-neck bottle was more than a new shape; it was a statement, a bold step forward that retained the brand's iconic status while evolving with the times. It was a huge success, and we were at the heart of making it happen.

PACKAGING CREATES OPPORTUNITIES

Packaging isn't only a necessity for protecting and transporting a product, but it's also a strategic tool that can either drive growth or hold a brand back. It's a source of opportunity, opening new doors for expansion, innovation, and increased sales.

One of the biggest opportunities lies in brand expansion, which drives revenue and growth, enhances product experiences, and creates loyalty and trust. Packaging enables brands to introduce line extensions, whether through new product variants, seasonal designs, or limited-time offerings. Kleenex, for example, tweaks its box designs for different seasons: winter themes in colder months, and fresh, floral patterns to boost sales in summer. Similarly, many brands tap into flavor trends, like introducing a pumpkin spice variant during fall, using packaging to communicate new and exciting offerings.

Beyond line extensions, packaging plays a critical role in launching entirely new brands.

Remember Tony's Chocolonely?

What about new brands operated by a massive parent company? Many consumers don't realize that Procter & Gamble owns an enormous portfolio of brands they created (like Swiffer, Febreze, and Cascade) or that Pepsi and Coca-Cola go beyond soft drinks (LifeWTR is a PepsiCo brand and Dasani is Coca-Cola's own bottled water). When done right, introducing new brands can be a game changer, allowing companies to compete in new spaces without diluting their core brand equity.

Another major packaging opportunity is to drive incremental purchases. Once consumers are engaged with a brand, the right packaging can encourage them to buy more. This could mean introducing a new type of pizza crust or a different take on a classic beverage, like milk (there's coconut milk, soy milk, almond milk, and more recently: oat milk), giving existing customers more reasons to stay within the brand's portfolio. Rather than always chasing new consumers, brands can focus on deepening their engagement with those they already have.

This mirrors how businesses grow either by acquiring new clients or increasing value from existing ones. It's the same in retail: Brands can either attract new shoppers or encourage loyal consumers to buy more, more often. Smart packaging strategy fuels both.

In the end, packaging isn't just about containment; it's about expansion, differentiation, and driving sustained growth. When brands get it right, packaging doesn't only reflect success, but it *creates* success.

RXBAR: STANDING OUT IN A CROWDED NUTRITION BAR MARKET

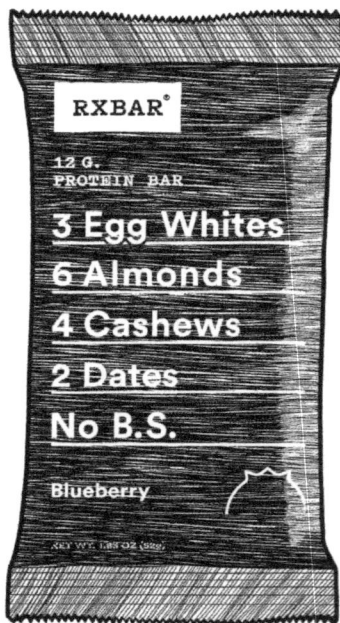

Before   **After**

The protein/energy bar aisle is oversaturated with competition. Between established brands like Clif, Quest, Kind, Pure Protein, PowerBar, and Think!, newer entrants often struggle to carve out a distinct identity.

Early on, RXBAR faced this exact problem. Their original packaging was cluttered with fruit imagery, generic design elements, and horizontal layouts that blend into the sea of competing bars rather than stand out.

But then came a bold shift in branding and packaging. One that completely repositioned RXBAR in the market and led to a significant increase in sales.

RXBAR's breakthrough came when they redesigned their packaging with a no-nonsense, minimalist approach that put ingredients front and center. Instead of showing fruits, indulgent visuals, or lifestyle imagery, the new design featured:

- A vertical orientation for stronger shelf presence
- A plain, single-color background to create immediate contrast
- The core ingredients listed in large, bold text (e.g., 3 Egg Whites. 14 Peanuts. 2 Dates.)
- A short tagline: "No B.S."

This design did 2 things at once:

- It cut through the visual clutter of the protein bar category, making RXBAR instantly recognizable.
- It reinforced the brand's value proposition of clean, simple ingredients and no unnecessary additives.

The shift in packaging wasn't just a design refresh; it better positioned RXBAR in the market. The minimalist approach turned into a brand philosophy, allowing the packaging itself to serve as a proof point of product transparency.[15]

The results? A dramatic increase in sales, with RXBAR quickly growing into a leading player in the protein bar category. Eventually, the brand's momentum led to its $600 million acquisition by Kellogg's in 2017.[16] This is proof that a well-executed packaging strategy can transform a niche product into a mainstream juggernaut.

RXBAR's success highlights a key principle of visual branding: Sometimes, the best way to stand out is to strip everything away. By removing distractions and focusing on what mattered most (the ingredients), RXBAR turned its packaging into a marketing tool that required zero explanation. Shoppers could glance at the bar and instantly understand what's inside, what's not inside, and why the bar is different from everything else on the shelf.

RXBAR proves that packaging isn't just a wrapper. It's a statement. When done right, it doesn't just complement the brand. It becomes the brand.

TRULY ICONIC PACKAGING

When people think of their favorite brands, they don't just recall the name; they see the packaging.

And we know that packaging drives sales.

Across best-in-class examples, the visual identity of a product is inseparable from the brand itself, and in many cases, packaging is what makes a brand iconic.

Coca-Cola is a perfect illustration. When you picture Coke, you likely see the red and white color scheme, the flowing script logo, or the hourglass-shaped bottle. Even if the label was removed or distorted (say, replaced with a generic squiggle), you'd still recognize it. That's the power of visual branding in packaging.

The same holds true for brands like Pringles, with its unmistakable can, or Starbucks, whose siren logo and green accents are instantly familiar. The soft blue and pink hues on Johnson's Baby Powder's white bottle are visual markers that immediately trigger brand recognition. This level of familiarity isn't just a by-product of marketing; it's a strategic advantage. The strongest brands use their packaging as an owned asset that reinforces trust, strengthens emotional connection, and extends into other marketing channels.

A red soda can instantly signals Coca-Cola, and a simple green-and-white mermaid silhouette gives away Starbucks.

A STRATEGIC WEAPON

Packaging drives sales. It is a strategic weapon, a storyteller, and an emotional connector. As Tony's Chocolonely proved, packaging can be a movement, not just a marketing tool. In a crowded $119.39 billion chocolate industry dominated by established brands, Tony's thrived while breaking all the rules. Bold colors, chunky typography, and a powerful story of social impact set Tony's apart, proving that packaging can inspire loyalty, create emotional bonds, and drive explosive growth.

But as powerful as packaging can be, it's also one of the riskiest levers a brand can pull. One misstep can confuse loyal customers or fail to attract new ones. Just as Tony's Chocolonely used packaging to stand out, other brands face the challenge of maintaining relevance without losing trust. The next chapter explores these challenges, diving into the complexities of packaging decisions and the high stakes that come with getting it wrong.

In an ever-changing retail landscape, where first impressions make or break a sale, the stakes couldn't be higher. Let's explore why navigating these challenges is mission critical for any brand looking to compete and win.

TL;DR: Packaging Is Mission Critical

- Challenge: Packaged goods brands work across some of the most competitive, margin-sensitive industries on the planet. In 2024, the global CPG market was valued at $2.299 trillion, and shoppers are bombarded with visual choices on shelves that make it hard to stand out, especially for new or niche players. In this environment, packaging has to do more than contain a product. It must capture attention, shape perception, and drive sales.
- Traditional Limitations: Packaging decisions have long been treated as aesthetic or executional rather than strategic. Many brands overlook the functional and emotional role packaging plays at shelf, resulting in missed opportunities to reinforce identity, attract trial, or deepen loyalty. When packaging misfires, the cost isn't just creative but commercial, as brands risk shelf invisibility, consumer confusion, or outright sales decline.
- Our Solution: Packaging is more than a business lever. Through behavioral observation and real-world testing, we reveal how packaging influences consumer behavior and commercial performance. From standout brands like Tony's Chocolonely to legacy icons like Heinz and Jack Daniel's, we demonstrate how smart, strategic packaging drives growth, communicates brand essence, and reinforces emotional connection.
  - Key Benefits:
    - Shapes perception and emotional response before trial
    - Reinforces brand identity and loyalty
    - Serves as a competitive differentiator at shelf
    - Connects advertising to the moment of purchase
    - Creates opportunities to expand, capitalize on premium assets, and innovate

- Impact: Whether launching a new entrant like RXBAR or evolving a classic like Heinz, smart packaging strategy transforms a visual asset into a commercial one. It increases trial, deepens loyalty, and drives measurable sales growth. In today's retail landscape, packaging is no longer optional: It's essential. And when done right, it becomes the brand.

Chapter 2.

THE CHALLENGES WITH PACKAGING

Before   After

In early 2009, Tropicana, a leading orange juice brand, undertook a significant packaging redesign for its Pure Premium line, aiming to modernize its image. The new design replaced the iconic image of an orange pierced by a straw with a minimalist depiction of a glass of orange juice. Additionally, the brand name was rotated vertically, and the familiar "Pure Premium" label was replaced with "100% Orange Pure and Natural." The cap was also redesigned to resemble the texture of an orange. This comprehensive overhaul was intended to refresh the brand's appearance and resonate with contemporary consumers.

However, the redesign led to unintended consequences. Consumers expressed confusion and dissatisfaction, with many failing to recognize the new packaging on store shelves. This disconnect resulted in a 20% decline in sales within the first 2 months, amounting to a loss of approximately $30 million. In response to the backlash and financial impact, Tropicana reverted to its original packaging design, restoring the familiar elements that customers had come to associate with the brand. The entire episode, including the redesign and subsequent return to the original packaging, is purported to have cost the company over $50 million.[17]

MAKE OR BREAK A BRAND'S SUCCESS

Packaging can make or break a brand's success. And in today's hypercompetitive retail landscape, the stakes are high, and getting it wrong is simply not an option.

We understand the challenges of packaging. But what about you, the packaging researchers and executives tasked with navigating the complexities of new projects? You're the ones making the tough calls, balancing consumer insights, brand identity, and business objectives, all while trying to stay ahead of shifting market trends.

Business isn't easy, but it isn't supposed to be; it's a full-contact sport.

As we began writing this book, we started with research. We talked with our clients and partners of all company and brand sizes, those new to packaging design and those with established careers at some of the world's leading brands. They shared their experiences, challenges, and lessons learned. We uncovered what it really means to be a corporate researcher, marketer, or executive in today's world, a world in which consumers are more unpredictable than ever, retail environments are more complex, and internal business alignment is crucial but at times elusive.

And what we heard was what we expected. The stories they shared revealed a landscape shaped by rapid change, fierce competition, and constant pressure to innovate. They spoke about the frustration of navigating fragmented retail channels, the relentless pursuit of relevance in the eyes of today's consumers, and the struggle to balance bold design with brand familiarity. They shared candid insights about what keeps them up at night and what drives them to keep pushing the envelope.

These are their stories. To protect their privacy, we've changed their names and the companies they work for, but the challenges are very real, and they will resonate.

Through examples and industry experiences, we will examine the tension between modernization and familiarity, the difficulties of standing out in cluttered retail and digital environments, and the internal pressures that make packaging decisions even harder. You'll come away with a deeper understanding of the true challenges packaging professionals face today and why strategic, insight-led design is essential for long-term success.

CELESTIAL SEASONINGS: CONFUSION AND DISSATISFACTION

Before

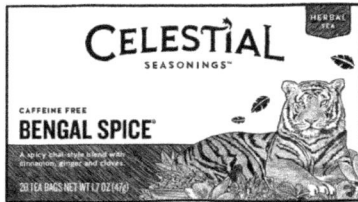

After

In 2015, Celestial Seasonings, a renowned tea brand, undertook a packaging redesign aiming to modernize its image and attract a younger demographic. The new design featured a clean, white background, updated typography, and a contemporary logo, while retaining some of the classic illustrations associated with their teas.[18]

However, long-standing customers expressed confusion and dissatisfaction, feeling that the new packaging lacked the brand's traditional warmth and charm. Some even reported difficulty locating their preferred teas on store shelves due to the drastic visual changes.[19] This feedback highlighted a disconnect between the brand's intention to refresh its image and the consumers' emotional attachment to the original packaging.

Recognizing the misstep, by September 2016 Celestial Seasonings decided to revert to its classic packaging. This return aimed to restore the familiar visual elements that resonated with their loyal customer base and reestablish the brand's identity in the marketplace.[20] The experience is a great example of the importance of aligning brand evolution with consumer expectations and the potential risks of abandoning established visual equities.

Understanding and preserving brand identity are critical. Drastic changes to familiar visual elements can alienate loyal customers and disrupt brand recognition. For companies considering a packaging redesign, this example highlights the necessity of thorough market research and consumer testing, so that changes align with customer expectations and maintain the brand's core identity.

Celestial Seasonings' redesign is a cautionary tale for brands considering significant packaging changes, emphasizing the need to balance modernization efforts with the preservation of elements that foster consumer recognition and loyalty.

REDESIGNING A BELOVED HERITAGE BRAND

Emma had just wrapped up another meeting with the creative team, a heated debate about the newest packaging design for one of the country's most beloved snack brands. The problem wasn't the team's creativity; it was the unspoken fear that hovered over every decision: Change too much, and they risked alienating their loyal, older customers. Change too little, and they'd never attract the elusive new generation of buyers.

The brand had been a household name for decades. Its bold packaging had long been a symbol of quality and trust. But the numbers told a different story. Market share was slipping. Younger consumers barely glanced at their products, instead flocking to sleek, minimalist offerings that spoke to their desire for simplicity.

Emma glanced at the redesign renderings on her desk, a bold departure from the original, with a simplified logo and a soft, gradient palette. The design was beautiful, modern even, but when they tested it, loyal consumers were puzzled, some even offended. "Is this the same one I usually buy?" one woman had questioned during a focus group. "This doesn't look like my favorite snack," quipped another steady customer.

Then there was the other side: ambiguous consumers. The ones who claimed they wanted modernity, but also tradition. The ones who bought anything new and flashy but would snap back to familiar choices when comfort was needed. Emma remembered insight from a recent study: Consumers were pulling out their phones in the aisles, researching on the spot. They wanted snacks that were good for you, natural, and trustworthy.

The packaging wasn't only that—packaging—it was the snack brand's entire identity. Could they keep the familiar elements while introducing something modern enough to capture the attention of young, experimental buyers? Or would every attempt to modernize take the brand's identity too far from its roots?

Her phone buzzed. A message from her lead designer: "Just got feedback from the new test group. Mixed reactions again. Let's discuss tomorrow?"

Emma stared at the message, knowing that every day spent debating design was another day the snack brand lost relevance. She couldn't shake the thought that one wrong move could fracture the brand beyond repair. If they alienated their loyal customer base, the backlash could be catastrophic. Distributors might start pulling them from shelves in favor of trendier, more agile competitors. Long-time retailers could question the snack's continued viability, and the brand's entire product line could risk being discontinued.

At the same time, if they failed to connect with new consumers, their competitors would seize the opportunity, gaining market share while the brand faded into obscurity. It wasn't just a packaging issue but the future of the snack brand. Emma knew that consumer loyalty was hard-earned, and once lost, it could be almost impossible to regain. She couldn't help but wonder if they were teetering on the edge of a brand crisis, one that could unravel decades of legacy and trust.

Refreshing an established brand without alienating its base or losing visibility is a scenario we've seen time and time again. It's one of the most common problems we help our clients solve, especially for established brands trying to modernize without breaking what's worked for decades.

What makes Emma's challenge so tricky is that her audience isn't neatly segmented. It's not only about younger shoppers versus loyalists. She's navigating what we call *ambiguous consumers*, people who say they want heritage but are drawn to modernity, who value trust but are enticed by novelty. That kind of shopper behavior is only becoming more common as the lines between categories, channels, and expectations keep blurring.

We have seen this challenge consistently across categories from beauty to beverages to personal care. The stakes are high. If a redesign weakens visibility or trust, brands lose ground fast.

This is the new norm. As consumer behavior becomes more

layered and harder to pin down, packaging decisions can't rely on instinct or internal consensus alone. They need to be grounded in what real shoppers do, not just what they say.

COLD AND COUGH MEDICINE WOES: MATT'S STORY

I worked on a cold and cough medicine project that was a complete redesign, focused on cleaning up the packaging and improving its aesthetics. But after it went to market, the new design system performed terribly. We did highlight potential risks, but when the news came that sales were down, it went straight up the chain.

Behaviorally was tasked to put together a postmortem to figure out what went wrong. The packaging had many positive aspects, but after digging deeper, we realized the brand had underestimated the importance of a core customer segment (older, loyal users) as well as a critical SKU within their lineup (which was responsible for most of the sales volume among this same cohort).

We had flagged the risk in the report, noting that the new design could significantly reduce purchases for the specific variant in the portfolio. Thankfully, our client had included that slide in his presentation, because he was able to prove he had given the warning.

The problem wasn't that the positive feedback was wrong. It was accurate and genuine. But the positive highlights combined with the strong desire to push the brand forward, after years of stagnancy, somewhat hampered the team from focusing on the reality of the risk involved.

This project confirmed that considering the complete story is a necessity to redesign successfully, whether that be intelligence on specific SKUs, audiences, or other contributing factors to a brand's success. One overlooked group or SKU can make or break a product launch, no matter how great the design looks across the entire portfolio.

Today, Behaviorally helps clients supplement their research even further, with solutions that provide extensive diagnostics to pinpoint in-market impact.

THE BATTLE FOR SHELF SPACE

Marisol, a small-brand manager, stared at her laptop screen. She had just received the latest sales report, and it was worse than expected. The vitamin brand she had poured her heart into wasn't catching on. Not in stores, not online. The numbers were painfully low, and she knew why. It wasn't the product; customers who tried it loved it. The problem was visibility.

Battling for shelf space in retail stores was a beast. The brand's minimalist packaging looked beautiful in the design studio but was easily overlooked in cluttered store aisles. Meanwhile, online, the brand was lost among countless competitors with more resources dedicated to online imagery.

She leaned back, trying to piece together the puzzle. She remembered a recent in-store observation: Customers barely glanced at her product. They seemed almost hypnotized by the big-name brands that dominated the shelf. Marisol's packaging was elegant but practically invisible compared to the colors around it.

And online, where brands don't benefit from brand blocking as they do in store, the muted approach was *also* lost in a sea of bright designs, some of which were better optimized for standout in an online environment. People were bypassing her product altogether. It was clear that online retail required a whole different strategy, one Marisol wasn't sure the brand could afford to implement.

An email came across. A message from Kristi, her social media lead: "New feedback from the online survey. Consumers love the concept but say they 'can't find it' in stores, or they 'haven't seen it' online. What should we do?"

Marisol knew they couldn't afford to waste time. The longer they stayed invisible, the closer they edged to being delisted. But every solution came with risks: Changing the packaging could alienate the few loyal customers they had, while investing in more targeted digital ads might drain their already stretched budget.

Representing a small, emerging brand trying to break into a crowded CPG category dominated by established players, Marisol's biggest challenge is determining how to differentiate her packaging so it stands out on shelf, communicates clearly, and appeals to both brick-and-mortar and e-commerce consumers. She also needs to understand where the opportunity gaps are, what existing brands are overlooking, and how to fill them without diluting her brand.

THE BALANCING ACT

Now, meet Steven, the global brand manager for a major international oral care brand. He was working on a new toothpaste tube design, which was sleek, modern, and undeniably beautiful. The problem was it looked completely out of place in half the regions they were targeting. Steven was caught in the middle of a branding dilemma that had no easy solution.

The challenge is deceptively simple: How can they maintain a cohesive, recognizable global brand image while also tailoring their packaging to local markets?

Steven remembered a recent meeting with the local managers. The Philippines wanted bold, vibrant colors to pop on crowded shelves. Thailand insisted on keeping the classic logo larger, while Vietnam requested a toned-down, earthy color palette. Meanwhile, headquarters was adamant that the core identity of the toothpaste brand remain intact as they expanded in Southeast Asia.

Business alignment seemed impossible. The global leadership team wanted a unified strategy, something scalable and consistent. Local markets, however, pushed back, arguing that without customization, the toothpaste wouldn't stand a chance against established local competitors. Some stakeholders wanted to innovate boldly, while others insisted on cautious evolution, fearing that drastic changes could damage the brand's trusted image.

Steven's phone buzzed, an email from his Southeast Asian lead: "Feedback from the latest shelf test. The new pack performed well in the Philippines but bombed in Thailand. Same product, same strategy. Totally different results. We're not sure what to do as we push into new markets like Vietnam."

They couldn't afford to get this wrong. If the global identity was too rigid, they risked losing regional appeal. But if they fragmented the brand too much, it would lose its identity entirely. Could they find a true balance between global consistency and local relevance? Or was this balancing act doomed from the start?

Global teams want efficiency and brand control. Local teams need packaging that works in their market. It's a constant push-pull.

We've seen this tension slow down launches, drain resources, and lead to designs that satisfy no one. And as companies expand into more regions, the stakes only grow.

The solution isn't more debate; it's having a shared understanding of how consumers respond. When teams can see what works and why, alignment becomes possible. Success is not about opinions or hierarchy. It's about clear, behavioral signals everyone can agree on.

LEADING THE WAY

The challenges of packaging are complex and ever evolving, shaped by shifting consumer behaviors, digital transformations, and the relentless pursuit of relevance. Yet amid these challenges lies an opportunity for innovation, a chance to break through the noise and connect with consumers on a deeper level. As we've seen, getting it right requires a delicate balance between aesthetics, brand familiarity, and messaging. Between digital presence and in-store impact. Between bold innovation and consumer trust. But standing out in a crowded market isn't just about adjusting to trends; it's about disrupting them. The most successful brands aren't merely reacting to change, but they're driving it. They're challenging conventions, rethinking traditional strategies, and embracing disruption as a powerful tool for growth.

At Behaviorally, we understand this because it's also in our DNA. We've built our reputation on redefining what's possible in research, leveraging disruptive methods to uncover deeper insights at a global scale, moving at the speed of today's business to help drive strategic decisions. In the next chapter, we'll explore the power of disruption in research and how our history of challenging the status quo has helped some of the world's most iconic brands survive and thrive in today's competitive landscape.

Let's see how disruption isn't just about breaking the mold; it's about building the future.

TL;DR: The Challenges with Packaging

- Challenge: Packaging decisions are high stakes and difficult to get right. Whether it's redesigning a heritage brand or launching a new one, today's market is unforgiving. Brands must navigate shifting consumer expectations, fragmented retail environments, and the pressure to stand out without alienating loyal customers. A single mistake can result in lost sales, retailer delisting, or erosion of brand equity.
- Traditional Limitations: Historically, packaging decisions have been driven by internal preferences or limited research insights that fail to reflect real-world complexity. This practice often misses key segments or SKUs and fails to account for ambiguous consumers who say one thing but behave differently. Without clear, behavioral evidence, teams risk making costly mistakes based on assumptions or isolated feedback.
- Our Solution: We address these challenges with behavioral products designed for real-world complexity. Our diagnostics uncover visibility and communication risks before launch. We help brands understand ambiguous consumers, balance global consistency with local relevance, and test pack performance in real-world contexts using predictive products.
  - Key Benefits:
    - Identifies packaging blind spots that can lead to sales decline or shopper confusion
    - Balances modernity with brand recognition by mapping consumer response to visual change
    - Supports global teams in navigating local nuances with real-world behavioral data
    - Aligns stakeholders around shared evidence to prevent internal debate and decision delays

- Impact: For brand leaders like Emma, Marisol, and Steven, our products provide the clarity needed to avoid costly redesign errors, connect with modern shoppers, and balance global ambitions with local realities. The result is smarter packaging decisions that protect equity, drive visibility, and win across markets.

Chapter 3.

THE ENGINE FOR PACKAGING SUCCESS

Nestlé was preparing to launch Vital Pursuit, a new line of high-protein, nutrient-rich meals developed to support consumers on GLP-1 medications and others focused on weight management.[21] The brand had a compelling product proposition including great taste, high protein, and essential nutrients but needed a packaging design that would stand out on shelf and clearly communicate these benefits. With plans for a nationwide rollout, Nestlé knew it had to get the packaging right.

Nestlé partnered with us to identify which pack design would best support their launch goals. They selected Behaviorally's Pack-Flash® option, our validation approach which observes shopper behavior and homes in on critical diagnostics to evaluate multiple design options in a realistic, in-context shelf environment. PackFlash was used to measure which designs captured attention, communicated key health and taste benefits, and ultimately drove stronger purchase intent. The goal was to choose a pack that not only looked good but performed measurably better with real shoppers.

PackFlash identified a clear front-runner: one design that effectively cut through the Sea of Sameness in the frozen aisle and conveyed the product's unique benefits. Specifically, it helped Nestlé pinpoint the pack that best communicated:

- High protein content
- Support for GLP-1 users and weight-conscious shoppers
- Appetite appeal and freshness

This design showed the strongest results across key behavioral KPIs, indicating strong shelf presence and shopper clarity. Our predictive insights gave Nestlé the confidence to move forward with this direction ahead of launch.

Vital Pursuit successfully launched across major US retailers in September 2024. It entered the market with a distinctive identity and a clear, research-backed design strategy. With our guidance, Nestlé was able to bring to shelf a pack that delivered visual differentiation, message clarity, and performance, which are all essential in a complex, competitive retail environment.[22]

A BRIEF HISTORY OF THE EVOLUTION
OF PACKAGING RESEARCH

Packaging research has come a long way from its early days of reliance on direct question-and-answer techniques. Over the decades, the industry has transformed by broadly embracing behavioral sciences, shifts in consumer behavior, and the rise of digital commerce. What started as a basic effort to understand what shoppers told us about packaging has evolved into a sophisticated field powered by in-context observation, AI-driven analytics, predictive modeling, and real-time consumer insights. Each decade brought significant breakthroughs that shaped how brands design, test, and optimize their packaging strategies.

To understand how we got here and why predictive research is essential today, it's important to look back at the key milestones that have defined the evolution of packaging research.

1970S: THE DAWN OF EYE-TRACKING
IN MARKET RESEARCH

In the 1970s, most market research focused on advertising, and packaging was still largely treated as a design exercise, optimized based on subjective preference or claimed feedback. Shopper behavior wasn't yet a priority, and few products existed to measure shopper behavior reliably.

Elliot Young, founder of Perception Research Services, said:

What the eye-tracking revealed was that shoppers' selection processes were happening very quickly—and many packages were never even seen or considered in the few seconds that each person spent at the shelf.

This gave us insights that we couldn't gather from focus groups or surveys—and it really highlighted the importance of shelf visibility, recognition and shoppability in driving packaging success.

Perception Research Services would later become Behaviorally. We were the first company to apply eye-tracking to test packaging designs, shifting the focus from what consumers *said* they noticed to what they *actually looked at*. This early move into behavioral observation helped brands go beyond surface-level perceptions and start exploring how visual hierarchy, color, and branding elements influenced real-world attention and decision-making.

It wasn't long before other packaging market research companies started to use eye-tracking technology.

1980S: THE RISE OF FOCUS GROUPS
AND QUANTITATIVE RESEARCH

Market research saw a shift toward scale and statistical rigor in the '80s. Quantitative methods began to rise in dominance, enabled by advances in automated survey processing. This allowed brands to gather structured consumer feedback at a volume and pace that was previously impossible, bringing more consistency to packaging evaluation. So we improved eye-tracking methods and overall data collection to embrace and promote quantitative testing.

At the same time, we were improving the products that made behavioral data possible. While early eye-tracking was still largely static, requiring participants to sit in place and look at fixed stimuli, we began refining the technology for packaging-specific research, evolving it from its origins in advertising testing.

By applying eye-tracking to packaging, we helped move the industry beyond the limits of claimed data. Our continued investment in behavioral technology during this decade marked the beginning of packaging testing as we know it: actionable, measurable, and anchored in real consumer behavior.

1990S: GLOBALIZATION, PRIVATE LABEL GROWTH, AND COMPETITIVE DIFFERENTIATION

As brands expanded globally, the 1990s saw an increasing need for packaging standardization across international markets. Global brands had to balance consistency with localization, leading to regional adaptations of packaging while maintaining a cohesive brand identity. At the same time, the rise of private-label brands introduced new competitive pressures, forcing established brands to rethink their packaging strategies. Copycat packaging became a major issue in this decade (and continues to the current day), with private-label brands mimicking successful designs to capture consumer trust.

In response, packaging research became more focused on visual differentiation, helping brands establish strong design cues to reinforce recognition and prevent consumer confusion. During this period, we also began formalizing behavior-based KPIs like visibility, findability, and purchase at shelf as action standards. These metrics, grounded in observed behavior rather than self-reported feedback, laid the foundation for today's predictive modeling, allowing clients to make consistent, objective decisions across brands and regions.

2000S: THE RISE OF PREDICTIVE ANALYTICS AND DATA-DRIVEN INSIGHTS

In the 2000s, packaging research took a major leap forward with the introduction of full-context shopping environments. Instead of evaluating packaging in isolation or with just a smaller set of competitive SKUs, we began simulating real shelves, complete with hundreds of products, to better reflect the complexity of in-store decision-making. This approach gave rise to a sharper focus on the First Moment of Truth (FMOT) and purchase transaction: the split second when a shopper encounters a product and decides whether to engage, explore, or move on. *Purchase transaction* means more than just expressed interest; it refers to a measurable, in-market sale. It's no longer enough to hope that packaging might influence behavior; brands now expect concrete proof that it drives real results.

Conducting these studies in person came with a cost, which often gave larger brands with deeper budgets a strategic advantage. But the benefit was clear: Only by observing behavior in realistic, full-context environments could researchers truly understand what stood out and what got left behind.

This decade also marked the growing use of predictive analytics in packaging research. Instead of just measuring appeal, we began to anticipate performance using observed behavior in context to simulate purchase behavior and optimize design. Packaging was no longer judged solely on looks or claimed preferences; it was now tested, validated, and refined based on how it performed in real-world conditions.

2010S: DIGITAL ACCELERATION, BIG DATA, AND AGILE RESEARCH

The 2010s saw an explosion of big data and digital research methodologies. Brands started testing packaging in virtual shelf environments, using online consumer surveys and behavioral simulations to gain faster insights. Research became more agile (we conducted research on research [RoR] studies with some of the world's largest CPGs, helping them confidently embrace online testing where full-context environments were essential), allowing for more frequent iteration and real-time feedback. Additionally, as e-commerce grew, brands had to rethink packaging for both physical and digital retail spaces. The concept of the Zero Moment of Truth (ZMOT), when consumers research online before making a purchase, became a critical consideration in packaging strategy.

2020S: AI, DATA DEMOCRATIZATION, AND THE FUTURE OF PACKAGING RESEARCH

In the 2020s, the insights industry entered a new era, driven not just by the emergence of AI, but by the integration of data across systems, platforms, and research modalities.

We've spent years productizing behavioral methods, digitizing packaging research, and systematically building the world's largest packaging performance database. That scale matters. Every test, every KPI, every shopper behavior turned into a structured data point. That foundation is what makes predictive insight possible.

AI is powered by data and acts as the connective tissue that allows us to combine large, diverse datasets including primary research, historical norms, and even select second- and third-party sources into a single, predictive model. It doesn't generate insights from scratch; it enables them by helping us identify and simulate behavioral patterns across packaging contexts. In our work, AI has 2 core utilities:

1. Machine learning enables us to productize.
2. Data orchestration allows us to connect first-, second-, and third-party sources in ways that increase precision and predictive power.

We use AI to enhance and accelerate our understanding—not to replace it. By integrating AI into our process, we've built a smarter, faster system that transforms packaging designs into behavioral data, analyzes that data in context, and forecasts performance with confidence. AI is not used to collect behavioral data or convert designs into training data for models, but it greatly enhances the power of our analysis.

The evolution of packaging research reflects a broader truth: Progress is driven by disruption. From our earliest eye-tracking studies to today's AI-enabled testing platforms, each advancement has helped brands better understand shopper behavior and make more confident decisions. But if the last 5 decades have taught us anything, it's this: Standing still is not an option.

RITZ: THE GREAT REPOSITIONING CHALLENGE

Ritz sought to strengthen its position within the competitive munching and flavor-forward snacking category. Specifically, the brand wanted to modernize the visual identity of its Toasted Chips subline to better communicate flavor, snackability, and relevance to evolving shopper expectations.

We deployed a multimodal research program to guide the redesign:

- Pack.AI™ was used first to screen initial design concepts and identify the strongest lead direction based on behavioral performance.
- PackFlash validated the final optimized design, quantitatively ensuring the new look delivered on visibility, communication, and conversion metrics.

The new packaging was launched successfully, elevating Ritz Toasted Chips as a distinctive snacking experience. The final design not only delivered on product taste and hand-to-mouth snacking expectations, but it also helped the brand reach new audiences and reinforce relevance in a crowded category.[23]

THE CHALLENGE OF CONTINUOUS INNOVATION

Continuous innovation in packaging research is essential, but it's also a challenge.

Brands that fail to evolve risk losing relevance, as consumer preferences, competitive landscapes, and retail environments shift at an unprecedented pace. Instead, brands must constantly test, refine, and optimize their packaging to stay competitive in a retail space that is more fragmented, fast-moving, and complex than ever before.

CPG companies don't operate in a vacuum. They play in an arena where the rules are always changing. From brick-and-mortar shelves to digital marketplaces, brands must navigate a retail ecosystem in which attention spans are shorter, competition is fiercer, and consumer expectations are higher. Packaging impact needs to go well beyond visual appeal. It must serve multiple functions across physical stores, e-commerce platforms, social media, and mobile shopping experiences.

The rise of omni-channel retailing has only amplified the challenge. Packaging design once needed only to stand out in-store must now also perform in search results, thumbnail images (to varying degrees), and influencer unboxings. Meanwhile, sustainability concerns, regulatory changes, and evolving consumer habits force brands to rethink materials, messaging, and design strategies at an accelerated pace.

What worked yesterday may not work tomorrow. And without a structured, research-driven approach, companies risk falling behind the competition. In a world where consumer attention spans are shorter than ever, brands must embrace AI-driven insights to remain competitive.

As you read on, you will discover how the field of packaging research has evolved from simple consumer surveys to a sophisticated, AI-powered discipline. We trace the historical milestones from early eye-tracking and focus groups to digitization and predictive modeling that have shaped how brands design and test packaging today. You'll discover why continuous innovation is no longer optional—it's a mandate—and how a modern, structured approach rooted in behavioral science, productization, and historical data, all unlocked and integrated by AI, gives brands the competitive edge they need. The rest of this chapter lays the groundwork for understanding how our predictive packaging engine helps brands win in an omni-channel, fast-moving world.

THE INDUSTRY RESISTED: WE DIDN'T

Yes, we just said brands must embrace predictive insights to remain competitive. And if your first instinct is to run for the hills, you're not alone.

The research industry has a long history of resisting disruption. Nowhere was this more evident than in the slow adoption of digital methodologies. Packaging research firms clung to the belief that in-person testing was the only valid way to evaluate consumer interaction. After all, packaging lives in the physical world.

The irony? Other disciplines, like advertising research for magazines and newspapers, transitioned online with impressive results. But when it came to packaging, many firms insisted the stakes were different. That resistance slowed innovation, keeping packaging research anchored in outdated processes even as technology made digital testing faster, more precise, and more predictive.

The longer that resistance held, the more the gap widened between what the industry was doing and what it could be doing.

We have never been content to wait for the industry to catch up. Disruption isn't just something we accept—it's the core of our identity.

That mindset led us to pioneer packaging eye-tracking, utilize full-context for behavioral observations, digitize our research platforms before "agile" became a buzzword, and productize our methodologies to drive the speed and scale needed for predictive modeling. In 2020, when in-person research came to a halt, we didn't. We continued our march forward with PackFlash: our already-existing, scalable, digital packaging research product that evaluated consumer behavior in context. It met the moment and pointed the way forward.

In hindsight, that was just the beginning of more to come.

We knew that digitizing was the first step. The real breakthrough would come when we combined our behavioral science expertise, productized research models, and used AI to structure and combine the data, as well as shop as a human would. That's what led us to build the predictive packaging engine that's transforming how packaging research gets done.

While others waited, we acted. While they stuck to the old playbook, we rewrote it.

WE CHALLENGE TRADITION

We have always recognized that packaging research techniques must evolve to truly capture how consumers interact with packaging in real-world settings; our approach has always been rooted in the idea that to drive better packaging outcomes, we must challenge market-research norms. Our belief in disruption is more than just a philosophy; it's a foundational principle that has shaped our methodologies for decades. It started when we pioneered the use of eye-tracking in packaging research. We consistently adopted technological advances of static eye-tracking techniques along the way, then moved to *mobile* eye-tracking research and embraced further digitization, including virtual shelf testing via desktop and laptop computers using webcams for accurate eye-tracking of full-shelf context environments.

In 2020, there was suddenly a need to rely solely on digitized packaging research because in-person studies were no longer available. Since we leaned into digitization in the 2010s and built PackFlash, we were already set up for online research when it became essential during the pandemic.

The product captures how consumers respond both instinctively and deliberately. By tapping into principles of behavioral science, using our proprietary productization methods to capture data and our world-leading database, PackFlash isolates and measures the drivers of real-world decision-making, providing insight into how and why consumers choose at the shelf.

PackFlash was a game changer in 2020, and as the speed of continuous innovation increases, it's time to flip the switch and disrupt the packaging research industry again. Rather than relying exclusively on existing methods, we've pushed forward by leveraging AI to build a predictive packaging engine to enhance our product offering. This started back in 2019, *before* the pandemic.

Market research and disruption should go hand in hand but

often don't. This belief is what has propelled us to redefine how packaging effectiveness is measured. We've developed a model that delivers fast and reliable insights, ensuring that brands can optimize their packaging with unparalleled speed and confidence.

A BOLD VISION FOR TRANSFORMATION: ALEX'S STORY

When I joined Behaviorally as CEO in 2019, I had a vision for full digital transformation, but like any major shift, my vision wasn't universally embraced. Many at Behaviorally had spent decades refining in-person research methodologies while we had (relatively speaking) begun to move away from those tried-and-true methods. It felt like a notably large risk to go "digital first" as it was a clear departure from what had made the company successful. The resistance wasn't just about technology—after all, the company had already pivoted to online products for a sizable portion of its research delivery. It was about changing deeply ingrained habits that had long favored physical testing environments prior to digital ones.

The COVID-19 crisis, while challenging, presented an opportunity—a chance to fully commit to digital research, rather than being held back by established methodologies. For us, this helped tip the scales to become digital first.

By 2021, we officially became Behaviorally, a company built on technology and behavioral science, culminating in digital-first insights. It marked a defining moment in our journey. This wasn't just a rebrand; it was a strategic shift that allowed us to disrupt the industry and redefine what packaging research could be.

Packaging research has always eventually adapted to technological advancements and shifts in consumer behavior, but the pace of change has never been faster than it is now. Behaviorally's now proven muscle for digital transformation has set us up culturally, and in terms of data capability, for further transformation in what will be a decade of even faster technology-driven change and growth ahead.

OUR NEW MODEL: A STRUCTURED APPROACH

Building our predictive packaging engine wasn't about simply following trends; it was about creating a system that could *accurately predict packaging effectiveness at scale.*

This system was built on 4 foundational pillars:

1. Behavioral Science: Grounded in decades of shopper insights and rigorous research into how people make decisions.
2. Productization: Built as repeatable, outcome-oriented tools, these products are designed for consistency, usability, and business impact.
3. Our Database: Powered by the largest and richest first-party packaging dataset in the industry, ensuring that outputs are both predictive and proven.
4. AI: Connected to datasets, including second- and third-party data, to make a better prediction.

Altogether, these pillars create our predictive packaging engine.

PILLAR 1: BEHAVIORAL SCIENCE

Behavioral science has long challenged the assumption that consumers make rational, deliberate choices when selecting products. Instead, research has shown that most decisions are driven by habit, impulse, and subconscious cues, a concept popularized by Daniel Kahneman's *System 1 Thinking.*

We embraced the teachings of B. J. Fogg and Roger Dooley, too, and developed our Benefits & Barriers model that helps brands understand what is working and what is not.

By studying actual shopper behavior rather than self-reported intentions, we ensure that the model's predictions align with how consumers behave in the real world.

PILLAR 2: PRODUCTIZATION

However, behavioral science–based data isn't enough; it needs to be formally structured to ensure consistency and scalability. This approach turned every study into a standardized data capture, allowing us to collect behavioral KPIs in the same way, across categories, regions, and test types. As a result, our database has grown exponentially, not just in size but in consistency, now representing years of clean, structured shopper data at shelf. This productized approach ensures insights are not only predictive but also repeatable and actionable, empowering brands to make informed decisions with confidence.

PILLAR 3: OUR DATABASE

In turn, productization brings a formal structure to our research process. We systematically gather KPIs critical to driving purchase transactions and continuously collect and organize data on how consumers engage with packaging. Over time, this has allowed us to build the world's largest database of shopper behaviors and pack design diagnostics, grounded in years of quantified metrics.

PILLAR 4: AI

This extensive dataset allows models using computer vision AI to identify patterns between shopping data and packaging design, measure success factors, and provide predictive insights that are fast, reliable, and cost efficient. The combination of historical pack data and AI-driven analysis enables brands to anticipate which packaging elements will enhance engagement, drive brand recognition, and increase sales.

We use regression models, convolutional neural networks (CNNs), and transformers to teach our machine to learn by example. By integrating behavioral science with productization; real-world data to provide not just a dependent variable in sales but also a point of view on elements such as brand and claim; and AI, we have created a predictive packaging engine that delivers real-time, forward-looking insights that help brands optimize packaging, win online and in store, and stay ahead in a rapidly shifting consumer landscape.

Despite decades of progress in packaging research, something critical was still missing: a truly predictive, scalable product that could be applied early in the process before costly design decisions were made. Brands needed a way to fill this upstream gap with fast, reliable, and actionable insights. That's what sparked the creation of our predictive packaging engine and, ultimately, our most advanced products.

In the next section, we'll explore the "secret sauce" behind these innovations: how we combined behavioral science, productization, and the industry's richest dataset with cutting-edge AI to build a smarter, faster, and more future-ready approach to packaging research.

THE SECRET SAUCE: POWERING OUR DATABASE WITH CUTTING-EDGE AI

The secret sauce behind our predictive packaging engine is how first-, second-, and third-party data are connected.

It's important to distinguish between the 2 key ways we apply AI in our system. First, we use computer vision AI to extract visual and textual elements from packaging designs, everything from layout and color to claims and typography. This allows us to transform visual packs into structured, analyzable data.

Second, we apply predictive analytics, a separate process that links this structured design data to historical shopper behavior and actual sales outcomes. This is the engine behind our products that use regression models to simulate how packaging will perform in market.

In short: Computer vision helps us understand what a pack is, while predictive analytics helps us forecast what it will do. This recipe has given birth to our new generation of products:

- PackPower Score™ (PPS): A single-number score using AI to predict sales impact.
- Pack.AI: A product that allows rapid, iterative testing at scale for packaging design.
- unPACKED: A report that decodes packaging drivers at the category level.

These products represent the evolution of our behavioral science expertise, proprietary productization, and world-leading database *powered by* cutting-edge AI.

All so we can predict sales driven by packaging.

With decades of behavioral insights and shopper research fueling the system, it's the depth of the data that matters, and now AI can be used to analyze, learn from, and apply that data in new ways. This is what makes the products we launch truly predictive.

Remember Emma, Marisol, and Steven from Chapter 2?

Our predictive packaging engine is perfectly equipped to solve their packaging challenges, whether understanding shopper behavior in a new region, accelerating early-stage design decisions, or aligning internal teams with clear, evidence-based insights.

In the next chapters, we'll show you exactly how.

TL;DR: The Engine for Packaging Success

- Challenge: Packaging research has struggled to keep pace with today's dynamic consumer landscape. The industry was built on manual methods, siloed data, and slow processes that couldn't deliver the speed, scale, or predictive accuracy required to guide modern packaging decisions. Brands needed a solution that could provide fast, validated answers before designs hit the shelf.

- Traditional Limitations: Research methods focused heavily on post-launch validation or subjective feedback rather than behaviorally grounded, predictive insight. Behavioral observation existed but lacked structure and consistency, limiting its value across regions, categories, and business functions. Most products were either too slow, too manual, or too isolated to be applied broadly at scale.

- Our Solution: We built a predictive engine designed to turn packaging decisions into performance outcomes. This system connects behavioral science, standardized products, the largest first-party packaging database in the world, and AI to forecast how real people will shop. With decades of structured behavioral data and machine learning models trained on observed shopper behavior, our engine helps brands make faster, more accurate design decisions.

  - Key Benefits:
    - Delivers reliable insight before launch using structured, scalable, productized research tools
    - Leverages the industry's largest behavioral database for consistent, cross-category benchmarks
    - Applies AI to decode packaging elements and predict purchase impact
    - Provides clear, decision-ready KPIs that link shopper behavior to commercial outcomes

- Impact: Nestlé used our engine to confidently launch Vital Pursuit, a new frozen-food line targeting GLP-1 users. By identifying the pack with the strongest clarity, appetite appeal, and on-shelf visibility, they entered the market with a distinctive, validated design. Our predictive insights eliminated guesswork and allowed Nestlé to execute a complex national launch with speed and precision.

Chapter 4.

IT ALL STARTS WITH BEHAVIORAL SCIENCE

In the early 2010s, the frozen entrée category took a big hit when consumers shifted to prefer holistic diets with whole and unprocessed foods. From 2013 to 2015, frozen entrée unit sales declined 7%.[24]

Lean Cuisine was heavily impacted by the fallout. The brand lost more than $400 million in sales between 2011 and 2016.[25]

To turn things around, Nestlé, which owns Lean Cuisine, knew it needed more than a product tweak or a new campaign. It needed a full brand repositioning, starting with packaging.

In April of 2015, Lean Cuisine launched the Marketplace line as part of a strategic overhaul. The packaging was designed to reframe the brand's identity from one of restriction to one of empowerment, health, and flavor:

- Sleek black background—Moving away from the dated "diet food" look, the new dark packaging evoked a restaurant-quality feel and gave the brand a more premium, modern aesthetic.
- Vibrant ingredient photography—Fresh, whole ingredients were featured front and center to visually communicate flavor and nutrition.
- Simplified layout—A cleaner, more contemporary design aligned with evolving consumer expectations around transparency and health.

This wasn't just a surface-level refresh. The new packaging became a vehicle for reshaping consumer perceptions.

The redesign paid off:

- At the beginning of 2015, the brand was in a double-digit decline in sales
- By July 1, 2015, Lean Cuisine Marketplace started to produce gains in sales
- The marketplace saw double-digit growth in Q3
- The brand increased sales by $58 million[26] the year following the redesign

While Lean Cuisine also supported the relaunch with broader brand messaging (notably its "Weigh This" campaign[27]), no major pricing or promotional changes were made, indicating the packaging redesign played a pivotal role in the turnaround.

The power of packaging to do more than sell a product. It can redefine an entire brand.

THE ROLE OF BEHAVIORAL SCIENCE IN MODERN RESEARCH

Behavioral science and market research haven't always gone hand in hand. In the early days, the role of behavioral science in market research was largely academic and anecdotal. Many studies illustrated consumer biases and irrational behaviors, but these findings were often treated as curiosities, interesting but not easily translated into scalable, repeatable methods. As a result, many firms viewed behavioral science as a novel theory rather than a foundational approach to understanding human behavior.

So, rational decision-making models were relied upon. One methodology from the 1960s, for example, assumed that if you asked consumers logical questions, you would receive logical answers. Research followed the classic marketing funnel, moving consumers from awareness to consideration to purchase intent as though people made decisions like machines.

But in practice, this assumption often fell short. What people said they would do did not necessarily match what they actually did. That gap between stated intent and real-world behavior is exactly where behavioral science quietly began making its mark.

Even before behavioral science was formally recognized as a discipline, its foundational principles drawn from psychology, sociology, and cognitive science had already begun to challenge the status quo. As far back as the 1960s, some marketers were quietly experimenting with ideas about perception, memory, heuristics, and emotional influence. While popularized research approaches focused on what people said, these emerging behavioral approaches focused on what people did.

We've always aligned with that behavioral lens, long before behavioral science became another key inflection point across the decades. And when "behavioral science" finally entered the mainstream in the late 2000s and early 2010s, we embraced the terminology because it captured something we'd already been doing: grounding research in real-world behavior, not just stated intention.

DISCOVERING WHO THE TRUE LOYAL FANS WERE: ALEX'S STORY

I once partnered with a beer company on a study that really drove home the importance of behavioral science in market research. They wanted to understand who was buying their product and whether their marketing was targeting the right audience.

At first glance, the survey data pointed us toward younger men. They claimed to drink the stout regularly and described themselves as loyal fans. But when we layered in the behavioral data, and real purchase behavior, the story flipped. Those same younger drinkers drank less than they reported.

Meanwhile, what about older men who said they were drinking less? They were the core customers, but they weren't reporting it in the survey. If we'd relied only on claimed data, we would've steered the brand in entirely the wrong direction.

That's the disconnect. People often don't (or can't) accurately report their behavior. It's not that they're lying; it's just that memory is flawed, and social perception plays a role. That's why we lean so heavily on behavioral science. It gives us the truth beneath the surface.

We don't just want to hear what consumers say. We want to see what they do.

THE SHIFT TO BEHAVIORAL RESEARCH

Even though we have been firm believers in behavioral science's critical role in packaging research from the beginning, it took the rest of the industry a lot longer to believe that self-reported data often diverged from actual behavior. Once the rest of the packaging industry began to recognize these limitations, there was a paradigm shift: a move toward behavioral science–based research.

SYSTEM 1 AND SYSTEM 2 THINKING

A major driver of this shift was the work of psychologist Daniel Kahneman, who introduced the concept of System 1 and System 2 Thinking in his book *Thinking, Fast and Slow*.

- System 1 Thinking: Fast, instinctual, and emotion-driven decision-making (e.g., Homer Simpson)
- System 2 Thinking: Slow, analytical, and rational thought processes (e.g., Spock)

Traditional market research was built on the assumption that consumers engage in System 2 Thinking, carefully weighing pros and cons before making a purchase. However, *behavioral science* revealed that most consumer decisions are made using System 1 Thinking, where impulse, habit, and subconscious factors play a much greater role than rational analysis.[28]

This fundamental understanding that most consumer decisions are made instinctively, not analytically, is the basis of how we have always designed our research.

We didn't want to force consumers into a rational mold, so we built a model that reflects how people actually make choices.

WHAT ARE HEURISTICS?

We often say that shoppers aren't reading, they're reacting. And at the heart of that reaction is a set of deeply ingrained psychological shortcuts known as *heuristics*. Heuristics are automatic, unconscious mental rules that guide human behavior. They're not flaws in reasoning; they're features. Our brains evolved to make quick decisions in complex environments, and heuristics are how we navigate the overload. This matters, because while we often hear what consumers *say* they want, what they *do* is shaped by heuristics.

There are hundreds of heuristics cataloged by behavioral scientists, some say as many as 400, but not all are equally relevant in a retail context. We focus on the handful that show up over and over again in packaging and shopper decision-making.

- Familiarity is one. The more we see something, the more we trust it, even if we can't explain why.
- Habit is another. Grabbing the same product every week isn't always loyalty; sometimes it's just being on autopilot.
- Perceptual salience or the "pop" factor explains why something that breaks the pattern (a neon pack in a sea of beige) gets noticed first.
- Nostalgia taps into emotional memory.
- Fluency refers to ease of processing (and leads to preference).
- Novelty sparks curiosity by breaking monotony.

These heuristics don't act in isolation. At shelf, they stack. A shopper might gravitate to a familiar shape, feel reassured by a brand they grew up with, and confirm the choice based on a quick, legible benefit callout. They're not comparing ingredients. They're not reading back labels. They're relying on heuristics to get in and out quickly.

We don't just acknowledge heuristics; we build for them. Our behavioral science framework is rooted in understanding how people make decisions, not how they *say* they do. That's why our KPIs (Be Seen, Be Shoppable, Be Seductive, Be Selected) map to real cognitive shortcuts. Be Seen is driven by perceptual salience. Be Shoppable ties to fluency and decision ease. Be Seductive leans into emotional resonance, where nostalgia, trust, and even flavor expectations come into play. And Be Selected is the final nod, the sum total of the heuristics stacking to drive conversion.

NATURE'S WAY: USING BEHAVIORAL SCIENCE TO OPTIMIZE SHELF IMPACT

 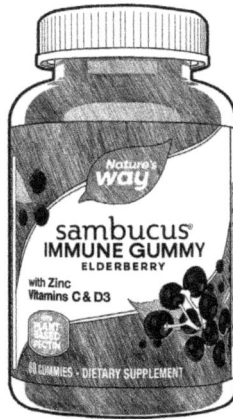

Before   After

Nature's Way, a leading natural supplement brand, was undergoing a full brand and packaging redesign across its portfolio. With new visual concepts in hand, the team needed to know the updated packaging would break through at shelf, clearly communicate benefits, and emotionally connect with both current users and new shoppers.

We partnered with Nature's Way using a multimodal research approach grounded in behavioral science. Leveraging our products, qualitative for early diagnostics and PackFlash for in-context behavioral validation, we measured how well each design performed in terms of visibility, navigability, and communication. At every step, we focused on understanding how real people behave at shelf, not just what they claim to notice.

The iterative process delivered a design that stood out and resonated. Compared to current and alternate designs:

- 86% found the new pack appealing
- The new design scored higher on purchase intent and emotional connection
- Shoppers found it more modern, vibrant, and easier to understand

Thanks to a rigorous behavioral science–led approach, Nature's Way landed on a final design that was not only beautiful, but measurably better, helping guide real purchase decisions in a complex retail environment.[29]

OUR BEHAVIORAL SCIENCE MODEL

Are heuristics a little too theoretical for you?

Rather than treating behavioral science as a theoretical exercise, we have always taken an applied approach. We have a history of building structured, scalable frameworks that can easily and consistently be used across research studies.

Our approach to packaging research has always been based on understanding the factors that drive or hinder consumer purchases, rather than simply asking consumers why they made a choice. Our highest-level framework, Benefits & Barriers, ensures that our research captures the impact of potential friction points that can create barriers at shelf, as well as assuring that cost-of-entry and point-of-difference benefits are effectively communicated. This helps avoid the pitfalls of relying solely on self-reported explanations, which are frequently unreliable due to memory gaps, social desirability bias, or incomplete consumer awareness of their own behavior.

To prove findings are actionable and repeatable, we developed our tactical framework: the 4S's, a structured system that organizes behavioral insights consistently. Rather than conducting isolated, one-off analyses, this framework provides a standardized method for evaluating packaging effectiveness by reducing barriers and promoting benefits, making it easier for brands to interpret results and apply learnings across different product categories.

FOGG, DOOLEY, AND THE PSYCHOLOGY OF PACKAGING

Modern packaging research doesn't only measure what people see. It's grounded in understanding why people behave the way they do. Two foundational thinkers in behavioral science, B. J. Fogg and Roger Dooley, have helped shape how we think about consumer behavior in the context of packaging. Their frameworks, while originating in broader behavioral design and neuromarketing, provide critical insight into how shoppers navigate choices in today's fast-moving retail environments.

B. J. Fogg, a behavioral scientist at Stanford, developed the Fogg Behavior Model, which asserts that a behavior happens when 3 things converge: Motivation, Ability, and a Prompt—or simply, B = MAP. This formula is deceptively simple but incredibly powerful:

- Motivation refers to the desire to act (e.g., the craving for a snack or the aspiration for a healthier lifestyle).
- Ability refers to the ease with which the behavior can be performed (e.g., how quickly a shopper can find, understand, and select a product).
- Prompt refers to the trigger that initiates the behavior (e.g., a pack design element, a shelf claim, a color, or even a well-placed visual cue).

In packaging, all components must be present. If a shopper is motivated but confused by the pack, the sale is lost. If the product is easy to understand but fails to grab attention in the moment, nothing happens. Fogg's model reveals a key truth about shopper behavior: The final decision is not just about pack aesthetics. It's about the holistic impact of the pack at the transaction.[30]

Roger Dooley, a pioneer in neuromarketing, adds another critical layer with his insights into cognitive ease. Dooley's work underscores that simpler experiences are more trustworthy, more persuasive, and more memorable. When packaging feels easy to understand, it lowers friction in the shopper journey. This doesn't mean every pack should look the same, but it does mean every pack must be fluent. A cluttered design, hard-to-read fonts, or a confusing architecture can all create "cognitive friction," pushing shoppers away without realizing why.[31]

Together, the thinking of Fogg and Dooley underpins one of the most important principles in packaging today: Successful designs must remove barriers and amplify benefits.

We incorporated Fogg's and Dooley's theories into our Benefits & Barriers framework. This framework simplifies decades of behavioral science into a single truth: When packaging makes the shopper's decision easier, it works harder for the brand.

BENEFITS & BARRIERS

Our solution to winning in the limited space of today's complex retail environment is a simplification framework that is predictive and data driven.

Successful packaging doesn't just look appealing. It actively works to guide consumer behavior. Brands must simplify the decision-making process for shoppers. One of the most effective ways to do this is by using our Benefits & Barriers framework, a structured approach to analyzing packaging success.

This framework helps brands identify and amplify the elements that drive purchase decisions while minimizing friction points that can deter consumers.

Benefits are the positive attributes of a product (as depicted by the packaging), anything that makes it more appealing, useful, or relevant to the shopper. These are driven by elements indicating superior quality, sustainability, convenience features, emotional or sensorial connections, or even a compelling brand story. To be effective, benefits must be clearly communicated (as viscerally as possible) and immediately recognizable, reducing the time consumers spend evaluating options.

Conversely, *barriers* are the obstacles that prevent a consumer from making a purchase. This could be unclear labeling differentiation due to poor element execution or architecture, leading to difficult shelf findability, or a packaging design that blends in rather than stands out. In the worst cases, barriers create frustration, cause hesitation, lead to abandoned purchases, or plainly dismiss a package from even being seen in the first place! By identifying and minimizing these points of friction, brands can remove roadblocks and create a more seamless shopping experience.

The Benefits & Barriers framework provides a simplified yet powerful lens for packaging optimization, allowing brands to diagnose where their packaging is excelling and where it might be failing.

When applied effectively, this approach ensures that products are not just seen but chosen, helping brands win at the shelf, drive conversion, and, ultimately, build stronger consumer connections. Of course, identifying Benefits & Barriers is only part of the picture. To operationalize behavioral insights at scale, we needed a repeatable structure, one that translates psychology into practical research design and ensures continuity.

THE 4S FRAMEWORK

Our 4S framework integrates core principles from Kahneman, Fogg, and Dooley. We built it to bring structure and predictability to packaging research. Each of the 4S's represents a critical stage in the consumer decision-making process:

- Be Seen: Does the packaging stand out on a crowded shelf or digital marketplace? If shoppers don't notice a product, it doesn't get considered.
- Be Shoppable: Is the packaging easy to navigate to? Consumers must quickly identify the brand, variant, and key benefits with minimal effort.
- Be Seductive: Does the design trigger an emotional or impulse-driven response? Strong visual and verbal cues encourage consumers to engage.
- Be Selected: Does the packaging convert consideration into purchase? Ultimately, the design must remove any obstacles to commitment.

This model is designed to bridge the gap between consumer psychology, behavioral science, and commercially useful insights, ensuring that packaging goes beyond generating appeal to drive purchase behavior.

Be Seen: Driving Breakthrough at Shelf

In a crowded retail environment, packaging must do more than just be visible; it must be salient enough to capture attention and stay in a shopper's memory. If consumers don't notice a product in the first place, they can't buy it.

Key Concepts

- Visibility versus Salience: Being seen isn't enough; the brand must stick. Shoppers are bombarded with visual stimuli, so visibility matters and so does recognition.
- Contrast Drives Visibility: The use of colors, structure, visuals, and typography determines whether packaging stands out or blends into the background. High-contrast designs (whether contrast stems from color, structure, or elsewhere) perform better in drawing attention.
- Full Context Is Critical: Packaging must stand out within its category, not just in isolation. A design that looks great on a presentation slide may fail when surrounded by competitors.

Examples

- Color Use in Branding: Coca-Cola (red) and Pepsi (blue) effectively use distinctive color blocking to drive instant visibility. Beyond that, elements of their respective designs also serve to drive instant recognition (e.g., Coca-Cola's hallmark script font and the timeless Pepsi Globe).
- Structure Enhancements: Brands like Fiji Water and Orangina use unique bottle shapes to stand out in cluttered beverage aisles.

Be Shoppable: Promoting Easy Product Selection

Once a shopper notices a product, they must quickly identify what it is, how it differs from other options, and why it's the right choice. Confusing or cluttered packaging slows down decision-making and may lead to a lost sale. In fact, our database shows that packaging that is easier to find, in the top 25%, is bought by 15 percentage points more on average than those in the bottom 25%.

Key Concepts

- Shoppers rely on color first (52%), visuals second (33%), and text last (13%). This means packaging must communicate key messages visually before relying on words.
- Differentiation versus Uniformity: A balance must be struck between brand consistency and clear product segmentation. Too much uniformity can lead to shopper confusion and missed sales. A lack of delineation can potentially do the same. There is a need for proper balance.
- Label Architecture: Strategic organization of packaging elements helps shoppers quickly locate the right product, simplifying the decision-making process and reducing frustration.

Example

- Pringles: Optimized SKU differentiation using a can for chips.

Be Seductive: Creating Emotional Engagement

Shoppers don't analyze every product they encounter. Most decisions are rooted in quick instinct based on emotional and visual cues. Packaging that evokes an emotional response can significantly impact consumer preference and purchase intent.

For example, among packages in our database evaluated for taste, the top 25% of "good tasting" are bought by an average of 27 percentage points more often than those in the bottom 25%.

Key Concepts

- Emotion Over Rationality: Consumers process visual and emotional cues far faster than they read product descriptions. The most effective designs instantly communicate a feeling or benefit.
- Simplified Hierarchy: Shoppers typically absorb only 3 to 4 key packaging elements. The most important communication points must be prominent and easy to grasp.
- Imagery As a Shortcut to Connection: Visuals are processed 60,000 times faster than text, making them a powerful tool for reinforcing emotional engagement.

Examples

- Baby food brands prominently feature infant imagery to trigger parental instincts, building trust and reinforcing security.
- Some pain relief brands leverage "body target" imagery, providing a quick, intuitive cue about the product's effectiveness and where it relieves.

Be Selected: Reinforcing the Final Purchase Decision

Once a shopper considers a product, the packaging must provide reassurance and eliminate hesitation, ensuring that they follow through with the purchase. Most decisions happen subconsciously, driven by habit, instinct, or brand trust rather than detailed analysis.

Key Concepts

- Eliminating Friction: Clear and intuitive designs to increase visibility and support effective differentiation reduce hesitation and make selection effortless.
- Reinforcing Brand Preference: Packaging elements that enhance familiarity and trust increase the likelihood of conversion. Brands that are in the top 25% of trusted brands in our database are bought, on average, 26 percentage points more than those in the bottom 25%.
- Subconscious Triggers Drive Selection: When products feel easier to use and provide convenience, or are more practical, consumers instinctively gravitate toward them.

Examples

- Sports drinks with ergonomic grips reinforce usability and brand preference in the moment of selection.
- Mouthwash bottles with built-in portion control simplify dosing, reducing uncertainty and making the decision easier.

By ensuring packaging is functional, emotionally compelling, and intuitive, brands can capture attention, build trust, and drive conversion, turning consideration into a final purchase.

The 4S's help brands optimize packaging for real-world retail environments. This structured approach allows brands to systematically evaluate and optimize their packaging, rather than relying on subjective feedback or individual preferences. It ensures that packaging aligns with how consumers shop (using System 1 Thinking) rather than how they claim to shop when asked in a focus group.

The 4S's in Packaging Design

Packaging strategy varies significantly based on brand size, as established brands must balance familiarity with evolution, while emerging brands need to fight for visibility, recognition, and their reason to believe.

Large brands rely on established visual equities that consumers already associate with their identity. When updating packaging, they must maintain the core essence of key brand elements such as color schemes, logos, and design structures to preserve recognition and trust. However, they also need to evolve to stay relevant, ensuring that changes feel fresh without alienating loyal customers. The challenge lies in introducing innovation while respecting the existing brand identity. A misstep can lead to confusion or loss of brand equity, as seen in cases where redesigns stray too far from what consumers expect.

Maintaining consistency in layout and brand element placement reinforces shopper recognition and makes the purchase decision easier. But sometimes, a bold design shift can signal new or enhanced product benefits and reframe how a brand is perceived. That's the balance between evolution and revolution in packaging design: knowing when to preserve what works and when to break the mold to drive reappraisal.

We regularly see how perceptual attention bias and familiarity bias shape shopper decisions often without the shopper realizing it. *Perceptual attention bias* happens when the brain focuses only on stimuli that match what it expects to see and filters out anything unexpected. In retail, this means that if a pack doesn't match what shoppers already associate with a product or category (its size, color, shape, or design architecture), it might as well not exist. Shoppers will literally overlook it.

For established brands, this can be a benefit. The consistent use of familiar colors and layouts reinforces shopper expectations, making it easier to be recognized and selected at shelf. This is where *familiarity bias* kicks in. Shoppers tend to stick with what they know, not necessarily because it's better, but because it feels safer. That comfort with the familiar gives brands a kind of cognitive shortcut. It reduces the mental energy needed to evaluate a choice and nudges the shopper to default to the familiar option.

But the reverse is also true. Challenger brands trying to break in must actively disrupt that bias. To overcome the perceptual filter, their packaging needs to be bold, novel, and attention-grabbing yet different enough to earn a second glance. Our methodology bakes this into the process. We evaluate not just if a pack is appealing at face value, but if it stands out enough to interrupt habitual scanning and earn a moment of shopper attention.

Through the 4S framework and Benefits & Barriers analysis, we can map exactly how these biases affect behavior. We ensure that designs account for these unconscious tendencies, either leveraging them to reinforce trust or disrupting them to spark intrigue. In either case, understanding and working with heuristics like these is essential to packaging that performs. Because at the end of the day, shoppers aren't just choosing products; they're choosing the path of least resistance through a very noisy shelf.

Small brands do not have the luxury of built-in recognition and must rely on bold design choices to break through the clutter. Since they do not yet have strong visual equities, design tactics such as distinctive colors, unconventional structures, and striking graphics can aid standout. The goal is to capture attention quickly and communicate a unique selling proposition with clarity and immediacy. A point of difference is critical for smaller brands, as they must work harder to establish a foothold in competitive categories.

While the 4S framework applies universally, the application of each S can differ based on brand size. At the core, large brands must refine and optimize, while small brands need to establish and disrupt. Paying homage to these nuances ensures that packaging attracts attention and builds long-term consumer loyalty.

BENEFITS & BARRIERS AND THE 4S FRAMEWORK: A PERFECT PAIR

The Benefits & Barriers model and the 4S's aren't separate tools: They're part of the same system, working together to help brands understand what drives (or prevents) shopper behavior.

At the highest level, Benefits & Barriers is the guiding lens. It helps teams identify why a pack is or isn't working: Are there barriers that create friction at shelf? Are there benefits that motivate purchase? These insights offer strategic clarity by framing the problem in behavioral terms. What's impeding or encouraging the shopper's decision?

The 4S framework sits just beneath that lens. It connects the high-level Benefits & Barriers diagnosis to the specific shopper experience: Was the pack Seen, Shoppable, Seductive, or ultimately Selected? Each "S" points to distinct behavioral dimensions that shape outcomes.

Then, at the most tactical level, we have metrics that evaluate how each "S" is performing. For example, if the barrier is not being seen, the 4S lens would frame this as a visibility issue, and the metric might be percent noting. If the benefit is strong appetite appeal, the 4S lens might diagnose this under Seductive, using metrics related to appetite, freshness, or emotional resonance.

Used together, this layered system of Benefits & Barriers, 4S's, and metrics offers both strategic direction and actionable insight. It ensures brands don't just know what happened, but understand why, and more importantly how to fix or replicate it.

Packaging gets one shot to win attention and drive action, and this integrated framework moves brands beyond guesswork into a world of repeatable, evidence-based success.

FROM SCIENCE TO STRUCTURE

Behavioral science gave us the foundation, an evidence-based understanding of how people make decisions. It taught us that shoppers don't respond to logic; they respond to cues. They move fast. They act on instinct. And they buy what feels easy, familiar, and rewarding in the moment.

That insight reshaped our approach to packaging research. We stopped asking consumers to explain their choices and started building frameworks that reflect how choices really happen. With Benefits & Barriers, we diagnosed friction and identified motivation. With the 4S framework and its accompanying metrics, we brought structure to the chaos by translating behavior into design evaluation metrics which fuel principles that work in the real world.

But theory is only powerful if it can be applied.

To make behavioral science actionable at scale, we had to go further. We had to productize our thinking and build solutions that could be used consistently across brands, categories, channels, and geographies. Then we feed that with the fuel of experience: all contributing to our proprietary database of real-world shopper behavior, collected and refined over decades.

Behavioral science isn't just theory; it's a lens that brings clarity to complexity. For Emma, who has to keep established customers happy while also attracting new customers, behavioral science helps cut through established assumptions and reveal what her consumers truly respond to, giving her the confidence to evolve an established brand. For Marisol, who is trying to get her small brand to stand out at shelf, it uncovers how behavior (not just stated preferences) is impacting performance in an oversaturated shelf environment, guiding her toward a design that works in the real world. And for Steven, who needs business alignment to move forward, behavioral science serves as a shared language by helping global and local teams align around a common understanding of shopper behavior. In every case, behavioral science is the anchor they need, reminding us that successful packaging doesn't begin with aesthetics or strategy. It begins with behavior.

Next, we'll dive into the final 2 pillars of our predictive engine (productization and extensive database) to show how to turn behavioral science into repeatable systems that drive confident decisions and predictable outcomes.

Because it's not enough to understand behavior. You have to build with it.

TL;DR: It All Starts with Behavioral-Science

- Challenge: In the past, packaging research relied too heavily on what consumers said, not what they did. Brands often made decisions based on self-reported data, only to find that real-world behavior didn't match. As the retail environment grew more complex and consumer attention more fragmented, relying on rational models or claimed intent became a risky and outdated strategy.
- Traditional Limitations: Classic research frameworks assumed shoppers made deliberate, logical decisions. But consumers don't analyze every choice at shelf. They rely on heuristics like familiarity, fluency, and emotional cues to navigate. Without a way to observe and decode these instinctive behaviors, brands were left guessing why packaging succeeded or failed.
- Our Solution: We replaced assumptions with observation. By grounding packaging research in behavioral science, we created models that reflect how decisions really happen. Our Benefits & Barriers framework identifies what drives or blocks action. Our 4S model breaks decision-making into 4 behavioral stages: Be Seen, Be Shoppable, Be Seductive, and Be Selected. These structured systems translate human behavior into actionable design insights that drive performance.
  - Key Benefits:
    - Replaces claimed data with observed behavior, revealing what truly drives choice
    - Identifies friction points that reduce conversion and elements that motivate purchase
    - Provides a shared behavioral lens for cross-functional decision-making
    - Simplifies complexity with repeatable frameworks that scale across categories

- Enables brands to optimize for how people actually shop, not how they say they do
- Impact: Lean Cuisine reversed a multi-year sales decline by using packaging to redefine its identity. Nature's Way used our behavioral products to land a design that was both appealing and effective.

And for brands like Emma's, Marisol's, and Steven's, behavioral science provides clarity, alignment, and a practical path forward. It helps them understand the shopper, build packaging that performs, and move confidently from insight to execution.

Chapter 5.

THE FOUNDATION OF PREDICTION

Before automation, before predictive models, before AI became the buzzword of the decade—there was the database.

Not a static archive, but a living, breathing system, quietly amassing hundreds of millions of observations on how real people interact with real packaging in real shopping environments. Long before the market shifted to AI and chat, we were building the industry's most powerful behavioral dataset. And today, that database is our single greatest asset.

With over 400 million recorded shopper behaviors, more than 160,000 designs and shelf environments tested, and 55,000-plus fully validated packs, this isn't just a big database. It's the most robust packaging insights engine in the world. It's deep. It's structured. It's behavioral to its core. And it's been built over years, not scraped from the internet or rushed into existence by market pressure, but carefully assembled through consistent primary research in partnership with the world's leading brands.

That scale matters, but what truly makes our database extraordinary is its consistency and complexity. Every study adheres to the same behavioral science framework. Every pack is evaluated across comparable KPIs. And every data point feeds into a structured system purpose-built for prediction. That means we don't just know what's working; we know *why* it's working, for whom, and under what conditions.

Brands had a need for faster, cheaper, and smarter packaging insights, and we didn't need to start from scratch. We already had the foundation. Productization isn't just about reducing costs. It's about scaling intelligence. And our database is what makes that scale possible.

STRUCTURE AT SCALE

Predicting what people will do at the shelf requires more than just sharp insights. It requires structure. That's why we took our behavioral science foundations and translated them into something brands could act on again and again: productized research.

By turning our proven frameworks into scalable products and consistent methodologies, we created something bigger than a single study. We created a system. One that doesn't just explain how shoppers behave but turns that understanding into repeatable, real-time insight at scale.

We didn't do it for scale alone. We did it to bring clarity, consistency, and confidence to every part of the packaging development journey from early design exploration to final go-to-market decisions. At the heart of it is our behavioral science framework and a world-class database of observed shopper behavior that was years in the making. Now, with AI layered on top, we can harness all of that insight to do something truly powerful: predict sales.

This chapter reveals how we turned behavioral theory into structured, scalable products through the power of productization. You'll see how a consistent, KPI-driven methodology allows us to deliver fast, reliable insights while building the industry's most robust packaging database. You'll learn why primary data collected through decades of consistent behavioral research is essential for training predictive models and how our database gives brands a distinct competitive advantage. Most importantly, you'll see how our approach sets the stage for the next chapter: using AI to scale behavioral insights with unprecedented speed and precision *in order to predict sales.*

PRODUCTIZATION: A SCALABLE, REPEATABLE METHODOLOGY

A key priority for us has always been simplicity and scalability. We focus on behavior and developing a clear, repeatable methodology that can be applied at scale: productization. This consistency in data collection is the foundation of our world-leading database and predictive modeling methodologies, which ultimately leads to reliable, fast insights over time.

By creating a structured and replicable approach to the way we collect data, we ensured that our data can be used to build robust predictive models, and we developed a systematic methodology that allows us to work at scale. Through productization, we have exponentially increased our database from 18 million behaviors in 2021 to 400 million behaviors in 2025. Every study contributes to a growing knowledge base, continuously improving our predictive capabilities and enabling faster, more reliable decision-making for clients.

By integrating productized research, we've created a system where clients can upload packaging designs and receive predictive analytics instantly to assess how well a package is likely to perform in market.

Our model evaluates packaging effectiveness across critical KPIs within our 4S framework:

- Be Seen
- Be Shoppable
- Be Seductive
- Be Selected

AI is only as powerful as the data behind it. What truly sets what we do apart is not just the structure of our methodology but the depth and quality of the data we've built it on.

WHY PRODUCTIZATION?

Productization isn't just a way to accelerate research. It's how we ensure clarity, consistency, and confidence across both client organizations and our own teams.

For our clients, productized research lends to easier global alignment. When every team is working from the same behavioral framework and KPI set, the interpretation and insights of datasets become immediately actionable. Consistent standards can be set to define the actions taken from various outcomes via scorecards that can be compared across brands, channels, and regions. Said differently, teams can speak a shared language. Productization supports consistent, enterprise-wide decision-making and makes it easier to benchmark performance, prioritize resources, and justify strategic decisions.

Internally, productization creates space for what really matters. Instead of spending time and effort building custom questionnaires through differing lenses that inevitably end up chasing the same principles (e.g., impact at shelf, communication of a proposition, etc.), we begin with proven templates rooted in behavioral science. This lets our teams focus on what really drives impact: digging into the data, interpreting patterns, and delivering sharper, more strategic guidance to let our clients focus on taking action accordingly. We don't waste cycles on reinventing methods. We spend them on making meaning.

Productization also ensures that every study we run contributes to a growing body of structured knowledge. More data means more fuel, which is used to make better predictions. We enrich our primary data with metadata; some of that metadata is extracted using AI.

In short: Productization makes our research faster, deeper, smarter, and stronger, along with making our insights more valuable on both sides of the table.

PACKFLASH: A DIGITAL GAME CHANGER IN SHOPPER RESEARCH

PackFlash is an example of productization; it's our proprietary, quantitative online research product designed to evaluate packaging in real-world shopping contexts. Built to simulate the dynamics of shelf environments, PackFlash allows brands to test packaging performance quickly and remotely, while preserving behavioral realism.

What sets PackFlash apart is its ability to capture both instinctive and deliberate consumer responses. Participants are presented with virtual shelves and asked to make selections in real time, revealing subconscious cues like visibility, as well as behaviors that tie to their decisions. Follow-ups include questions focused on visceral reactions tied to appeal and time-pressured exercises in competitive context, followed by probing of deliberate processing, such as perceptions of quality, relevance, and brand fit. This layered approach provides a more holistic view of how packaging performs across the full spectrum of shopper behavior.

Underpinning the product is our deep expertise in behavioral science, combined with years of productization experience and a robust proprietary database. This fusion enables PackFlash to deliver findings that go beyond surface-level preferences, uncovering the underlying drivers of choice that truly predict purchase behavior.

PackFlash doesn't deliver only speed and realism; it delivers accuracy. What makes clients return to this product again and again isn't just the respondent experience (though we work to optimize that continually); it's the predictive precision. That's the real differentiator. PackFlash is powered by a productized framework and connected to the world's most robust packaging behavior database. While other products may innovate on interface or UX, our competitive edge is clarity: accurate predictions grounded in real-world behavior. In the end, it's not about who can make testing feel easiest. It's about who can show what works, and why, before a single pack hits the shelf.

The importance of PackFlash was especially evident in 2020. As the pandemic disrupted in-person research methodologies, PackFlash enabled our team to adapt immediately without sacrificing rigor, speed, or behavioral validity. It wasn't just a substitute for in-store testing; it was a scalable, digital-native product that became a cornerstone of how packaging research could move forward in a remote-first world. For many of our clients, PackFlash became the gateway into more agile, AI-powered products that followed.

CHOBANI FIT: STANDING OUT IN A CROWD

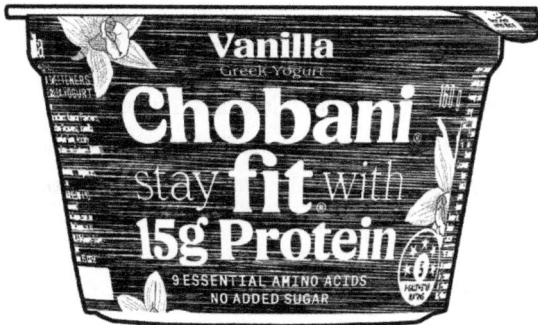

Chobani Fit faced a classic challenge in the fast-growing, protein-forward yogurt category. As new competitors entered the space with bold claims and eye-catching packs, Chobani needed to evolve its design strategy to better highlight its functional benefits and keep pace with shifting consumer expectations.

The goal? Attract new audiences, stand out on shelf, and clearly communicate why Chobani Fit was the superior choice.

To validate its new design system and ensure the pack communicated effectively against the competition, Chobani partnered with us to run a PackFlash study. This research provided insight into how well the updated packaging performed across 3 key behavioral drivers: visibility, findability, and purchase. Additional diagnostics also revealed how clearly the pack communicated its key points of difference (PODs) in a cluttered retail environment.

The results were definitive: The new design delivered. PackFlash gave the team the confidence to move forward, with consumer-validated evidence showing that the redesign improved not only shopper attention but also functional communication, helping Chobani Fit break through on shelf.

Post-launch, the results spoke for themselves. Chobani Fit saw 72% value growth versus the prior year in Australia, which is clear proof that behavioral insights, when paired with bold design decisions, can drive measurable business outcomes.

The combination of our behavioral science models builds our predictive engine. Now, let's take a look at what fuels PackFlash and all of our predictive models: our historical database.[32]

OUR MARKET-LEADING, HISTORICAL DATABASE

At the core of our predictive packaging engine is our proprietary, world-leading database, an unparalleled repository of behavioral data collected through decades of consistently executed research. This isn't generic or crowdsourced data. It's primary data captured from real shoppers in real decision-making moments, across categories, channels, and global markets and through the years.

This scale and specificity of data is what makes our predictive models more robust, reliable, and accurate than anything else in the industry.

Unlike firms that rely on secondary data, synthetic data, or generic AI models trained on publicly available sources, we made sure our AI is grounded in packaging-specific primary behavioral data. Every design our AI evaluates is compared against tens of thousands of similar designs already tested and observed through actual shopper interactions. Our models recognize patterns in proven behavior, predicting outcomes with precision before a product ever hits the shelf.

This level of consistency offers tremendous benefits for brands. Because every data point in our database is collected using the same behavioral frameworks, it allows for apples-to-apples comparisons across studies, markets, and time. Brands can confidently benchmark their designs against category-specific norms, identify patterns in consumer response, and make decisions based on historical precedent.

Our database also supports a more strategic approach to research planning. Instead of starting from scratch with every project, brand teams can leverage existing diagnostics and proven KPIs that align with their objectives. This accelerates timelines, reduces the need for custom questionnaires, and frees up time for higher-order thinking, allowing both clients and researchers to focus on insight generation and decision-making rather than data wrangling. It's not just about speed. It's about creating the space for smarter, more informed strategy.

Because our data is structured and collected using consistent methodologies over time, we can train AI models that identify what drives real-world purchase decisions—not just what consumers say they'll do, but what they actually do.

This gives the clients we work with a significant edge:

- Benchmarking power from the industry's largest database of packaging performance
- Access to pretrained, category-specific AI models ready to predict the performance of new packaging with speed and confidence
- Validated insights, measured against industry-standard performance metrics like RMSE (Root Mean Square Error) and NMAE (Normalized Mean Absolute Error), ensuring forecasts match real-world outcomes

This is the real advantage: not just AI, but AI powered by *the* most comprehensive packaging database in the world. It's what turns insights into action and predictions into proven results.

Looking ahead, AI will continue to evolve, enhancing the speed, precision, and depth of predictive insights. However, as brands and researchers integrate AI into their workflows, the importance of proprietary, high-quality behavioral data will only grow. AI is an extraordinary product, but in packaging research, the real power comes from the data behind it.

Why does proprietary data matter?

Our construct is built on decades of applied expertise.

Our models are grounded in cumulative behavioral knowledge, developed over years of consistent research and refined through direct partnerships with the world's leading brands.

Human expertise is baked into every layer: from how we designed our frameworks, to how we selected the most predictive KPIs, to how our teams interpret model outputs in context. The result is a predictive engine that does more than run on data; it is trained on consumer data in supervised learning. AI is built by data scientists with the counsel and knowledge of pack experts.

O ORGANICS—REPOSITIONING
THROUGH PREDICTIVE DESIGN

O Organics had established itself as a trusted organic brand but saw an opportunity to strengthen its visual identity and reposition its packaging to better communicate product benefits. The challenge was twofold: evolve the brand to stay competitive while retaining the equity it had built with loyal customers.

We applied our productized research methodology to streamline the process and ensure repeatable, scalable insights. Using PackFlash, we conducted an initial screening of multiple design concepts, leveraging our historical database of shopper behavior to benchmark performance and identify key optimization areas. Because our products are standardized and rooted in behavioral science, we were able to iterate rapidly and refine the strongest design routes. A second round of PackFlash testing validated the updated design before launch.

The redesigned pack launched in 2023 and immediately delivered strong results:

- 20% increase in perceived quality
- 30% lift in findability on shelf
- 39% stronger fit with the brand
- 50% decrease in perceptions of generic appearance

Our productized solutions, built on decades of real shopper behavior, allowed O Organics to confidently reposition without overextending timelines or budgets. The database didn't just inform the strategy. It made it scalable, repeatable, and grounded in what works.[33]

THE FOUNDATION MATTERS: UNDERSTANDING DATA

As AI becomes more deeply embedded in packaging research, one thing remains clear: The quality of the data behind the model makes all the difference. To understand why our approach is so effective, it's helpful to clarify the key distinctions between primary and secondary data, and between non-synthetic and synthetic data.

PRIMARY VERSUS SECONDARY DATA

Primary data is collected directly from research participants for a specific purpose. It includes behavioral observations, survey responses, virtual shelf tests, and other firsthand methods that reflect what shoppers do in context. This data is often highly structured, targeted, and collected using consistent frameworks making it especially useful for identifying behavioral patterns and measuring change over time.

Secondary data refers to information originally gathered for a different purpose such as third-party research, syndicated sources, or internal sales reports and then repurposed for new analyses. It can be helpful for context, benchmarking, or enrichment, especially when combined with more targeted datasets.

Both types of data have value in AI applications. The key is understanding their origin, structure, and suitability for the task at hand.

A core differentiator of our approach is the ability to link first-party behavioral data, collected in controlled, observed research environments, with second- and third-party data sources such as sales performance. This integration enables models that not only explain shopper behavior but connect it directly to business outcomes.

NON-SYNTHETIC VERSUS SYNTHETIC DATA

Non-synthetic data comes from real-world consumer interactions. It includes observed behavior, responses from studies, and actions taken in both physical and digital environments. It reflects actual decisions made by real people, offering a high degree of reliability when modeling shopper behavior.

Synthetic data, on the other hand, is artificially generated to resemble real data. It's often used to augment small datasets, simulate rare scenarios, or test models when access to real-world data is limited. When created responsibly, especially from well-cleaned, high-quality inputs, synthetic data can play a valuable role in enhancing model training or extending the analytical reach of a study.

Synthetic data can be particularly useful in digital and e-commerce contexts, where observed behavior is harder to collect directly.

Both approaches have their place. The key is knowing when to use synthetic data to extend insights and when to rely on non-synthetic data to ensure authenticity and grounding in actual consumer behavior.

By working with a range of data types, researchers can build models that are both scalable and grounded. Our strength lies in the models' ability to combine decades of structured behavioral insights with flexible, forward-looking products that adapt to the needs of each project. Whether working with hard-to-reach segments, broad category studies, or the rapid-fire and dynamic e-commerce environment, the goal remains the same: delivering insights that reflect how real people make real decisions.

By combining structured behavioral observations, outcome-linked performance data, and synthetic augmentation where appropriate, we can build models that are both evidence-based and extensible across retail environments.

BECAUSE WE HAVE THE RIGHT
DATABASE: ALEX'S STORY

A vitamin company we partnered with faced a classic multinational challenge: how to modernize a global brand without losing trust or recognition. Their team was starting a large-scale redesign and needed to evaluate the strength and adaptability of their brand mark across dozens of markets.

We had a solution because we had the right database.

Our structured, behavioral dataset built from decades of global packaging research became the foundation. Instead of reinventing the wheel market by market, we tapped into our database to identify what makes a brand mark succeed across geographies. Then, using AI as a modeling engine, we simulated design performance across shopper types, retail contexts, and cultural nuances.

This wasn't about skipping research. It was about amplifying it. The database allowed us to replace redundant testing with predictive insight, giving the brand team a cohesive view of how their packaging would perform worldwide. The result? A streamlined process, a unified creative strategy, and faster alignment across global teams.

When the data is deep enough and structured correctly, it doesn't just support global consistency. It makes it possible.

A NEW ERA OF PREDICTIVE PACKAGING RESEARCH

Productization gave us the structure. Our database gave us the scale. But structure and scale alone aren't enough. To meet the demands of today's fast-paced, high-stakes retail environments, brands need insights that are grounded in behavioral science and delivered with unprecedented speed, accuracy, and foresight.

That's where machine learning comes in.

Everything we've built, from our frameworks to our research

execution to our database, has been deliberately designed to fuel a new era of predictive packaging research. One where AI works directly with our database to make precise predictions. One where decision-making isn't just faster, but smarter. One where brands can evaluate designs not in weeks but in minutes and do so with the confidence that their choices are backed by real shopper behavior.

Looking ahead, our productized tools and behavioral database could play a pivotal role in helping Emma, Marisol, and Steven navigate their next big decisions.

For Emma, the ability to test and compare against a structured archive of similar designs means she could approach her heritage brand's refresh with clarity and confidence. Marisol, facing pressure to move fast in a crowded category, could rely on agile, productized diagnostics to quickly surface what's working and what's not without slowing down momentum. For Steven, whose world is defined by global complexity, our consistent KPIs and standardized research templates could help align teams across regions without sacrificing local nuance. Productization and the database aren't just about speed or structure. They're about giving decision-makers a smarter, more connected way to act.

We'll explore how our predictive products (Pack.AI and PPS) work, what makes them different, and how they're changing the game for packaging research. Because the future of packaging isn't just data driven. It's predictive, behavioral, and already here.

TL;DR: The Foundation of Prediction

- Challenge: As brands demanded faster, more precise packaging insights, most researchers found themselves unprepared. The industry lacked structured, scalable, behavior-based data capable of powering predictive models. The research approaches didn't deliver the speed and accuracy brands now needed.

- Traditional Limitations: Without a structured database of real-world shopper behavior, most predictive efforts fell short. Brands tried to retrofit insights from ad testing, focus groups, or synthetic data sources, but these lacked the depth, consistency, and packaging-specific rigor required to simulate true consumer decision-making. Data was either unstructured, too narrow, or collected without consistency across studies.

- Our Solution: We spent decades building the industry's most robust behavioral packaging database. With over 400 million behavioral observations collected through consistent methodologies, this dataset serves as the foundation for prediction. By productizing research through products like PackFlash, we created structured, repeatable methods to collect behavioral KPIs at scale. These feed our predictive models and enable fast, reliable insights that match real-world performance.
  - Key Benefits:
    - Consistent behavioral data across over 160,000 designs and 55,000 validated packs
    - Scalable products like PackFlash that simulate real shelf environments and collect instinctive and deliberate responses
    - Fast, AI-ready diagnostics built on years of primary research, not synthetic substitutes

- Clarity and alignment across global teams through shared KPIs and frameworks
- The ability to compare performance over time, across categories, and between markets using structured benchmarking
- Impact: Chobani Fit used PackFlash to validate a design that drove a 72% sales growth in Australia. O Organics repositioned with confidence, gaining clarity, findability, and stronger brand fit. A global vitamin brand modernized with speed by tapping into our structured database to simulate design success across regions. These stories show how productization and a deep behavioral database empower brands to move fast, act smart, and predict outcomes before they hit the shelf.

Chapter 6.

DELIVERING SPEED, SCALE, AND VALUE

Colgate was preparing to launch a new toothpaste innovation: Total Plaque Pro Release. The product promised advanced plaque-fighting benefits, but in a crowded oral care aisle filled with similar claims, the pack needed to do more than just look good. It had to capture attention, clearly communicate the benefit, and convert that attention into purchase.

We used Pack.AI to evaluate a range of design directions, testing each one across key behavioral KPIs: visibility, shoppability, purchase, and desirability. The goal wasn't just to pick the best-looking design; it was to understand what worked, what didn't, and why.

By leveraging AI, we were able to do this quickly and for a fraction of the cost.

One design quickly rose to the top. Featuring a bold, holographic emblem and a vivid, benefit-led aesthetic, it struck the right balance between shelf breakthrough and clarity. Our behavioral analysis precisely identified the drivers of performance, as well as a few subtle communication gaps that we worked with Colgate to refine.

The final design launched in 2023 and quickly stood out in market, earning strong consumer response and winning *Allure*'s "Best of Beauty" award. Most importantly, it achieved what every CPG brand wants: a package that sells the product.

Colgate's success with Total Plaque Pro Release is a powerful example of how behavioral insight and predictive testing can elevate even the most established brands.[34]

THE TRANSFORMATIVE POWER OF PREDICTIVE AI IN PACKAGING RESEARCH

Predictive AI is revolutionizing packaging research by continuing to solve against the ever-present desire to be faster, cheaper, and better, further combating slow timelines, high costs, and inadequate approaches.

It helps brands perform research at the same rate they conduct business.

In the past, in-person studies often took 8 to 12 weeks to complete; there were logistical hurdles like physical test setups, recruitment, and manual data collection. And, of course, high costs. Digital methodologies accelerated the timeline: first to weeks, and now, with machine learning, to minutes. By leveraging automation, virtual shelf testing, and real-time analytics, brands can now test, iterate, and optimize packaging faster than ever before.

But speed is only part of the story. Predictive AI also makes packaging research more affordable, inclusive, and accessible. Companies can conduct more studies within the same budget, maximizing the volume and value of insights without increasing spending.

Predictive AI also allows us to reach a wider and more representative range of consumers including segments that are typically hard to reach. By combining digital scale with structured behavioral frameworks, we're able to draw from a more diverse set of sources, expanding our reach without compromising on rigor. Crucially, everything is still rooted in our behavioral database built over decades of research.

Perhaps most importantly, AI-driven insights are more reliable now. We trained our AI on decades of consistent, structured shopper behavior data, which grounds predictions in real-world outcomes. This gives our clients confidence. The result? A more agile, efficient, and evidence-based approach to packaging development. Brands can move quickly, make smarter decisions, reduce risk, and stay ahead of the competition in an increasingly fast-paced retail environment.

In the coming pages, you'll learn how predictive AI is reshaping packaging research by delivering faster insights, scalable testing, and precise predictions rooted in real shopper behavior. We'll explore how a structured database, behavioral science framework, and proprietary products like PPS and Pack.AI work together to forecast packaging performance and drive sales impact. You'll also see how AI enhances qualitative research, and how our unPACKED reports offer strategic, category-level clarity. From pixel-level design diagnostics to scalable productization, this chapter unpacks the products and thinking that enable smarter, faster, and more confident packaging decisions.

AI ANALYTICS IN PACKAGING RESEARCH

The introduction of AI has transformed packaging research by making it more predictive, data driven, and precise. Instead of relying solely on stated opinions, AI models can analyze patterns in vast datasets of real shopper behavior to determine what truly drives engagement and purchase decisions. We have built a predictive engine specifically for this purpose, integrating behavioral science, productization, vast datasets, and AI into a scalable system that uncovers what makes packaging successful. This evolution allows researchers to leverage historical shopper data in entirely new ways.

Some of AI's most valuable applications in packaging research include:

- Identifying patterns in shopper behavior: AI detects subtle trends in how consumers interact with packaging such as what they notice first, what holds their attention, and what ultimately drives purchase decisions.
- Analyzing packaging elements to turn design into data: AI can systematically evaluate color, shape, text placement, and other design factors with precision and consistency.
- Predicting the effectiveness of design changes: AI allows brands to test packaging updates virtually, forecasting whether

a tweak in typography, a color adjustment, or a shape variation will improve impact. It can go further and combine shopper data and design data across thousands of packaging designs and pinpoint which visual executions lead to higher sales in seconds.

- Dissecting brand and claim performance: AI enables researchers to isolate and analyze the impact of brand cues and product claims, such as "high protein" or "organic," across thousands of designs. This emerging capability helps identify which brand assets and messages resonate most with shoppers and contribute to sales, offering a meaningful competitive advantage as the models continue to improve.

AI's role in modern packaging research goes beyond just identifying trends; it breaks down packaging at the pixel level. Through computer vision technology, AI can detect brand marks, fonts, colors, visuals, text placement, and structural elements, analyzing how these factors influence consumer response. It can measure the size and relationship of different elements on a package, evaluating if they are executed and prioritized effectively. By combining this design-level codification and analysis with behavioral data, AI reveals what truly drives shopper transactions rather than relying on assumptions or subjective feedback.

Despite AI's technical advancements, behavioral science remains at the heart of packaging research. AI alone cannot explain why consumers react in a certain way to packaging. It simply identifies and predicts patterns. Our approach ensures that AI-driven insights are always framed within the context of human decision-making, making research not only faster and more precise but also deeply rooted in how consumers think and behave. As AI continues to evolve, its role in packaging research will only expand, but one thing remains clear: The best insights come from combining cutting-edge technology with a deep understanding of consumer psychology. For us, AI isn't just a tool; it's a catalyst for unlocking the full potential of behavioral data assets. Years of digital research have produced an extensive dataset of how consumers interact with packaging in real-world environments. With AI, those insights can now be systematized, scaled, and applied in ways that were previously impossible.

By analyzing patterns across hundreds of millions of packaging data points, AI allows us to identify what drives consumer decisions, not just what people claim influences them. This shift enhances the precision of market research, enabling brands to refine their packaging before costly missteps occur in market.

CLARIFYING A VALUE PROP: MATT'S STORY

A very well-known coffee creamer brand operated in a highly saturated category (coffee creamers) with a complicated mix of product claims (nut-based, plant-based, dairy-free, etc.). This made shelf communication uniquely difficult. Not only did the brand need to stand out on a crowded shelf, but it also had to clarify its specific proposition in a landscape where variants and claims could easily blur together.

The brand's specific value proposition centered on natural, clean ingredients and plant-based simplicity. As part of the coffee creamer's portfolio, the brand was positioned as the better-for-you alternative, offering nondairy and dairy options made without artificial flavors, colors, or preservatives.

Key differentiators included:

- Plant-based varieties like almond, oat, and coconut milk creamers
- Simple ingredient lists compared to heavily processed competitors
- Emphasis on natural indulgence without sacrificing taste

This positioned the brand at the intersection of health-consciousness and coffee ritual, targeting shoppers looking for a creamer that aligned with wellness goals and ingredient transparency.

They partnered with us to benchmark packaging performance using PackPower Score. The brand needed a way to quickly and consistently understand how its pack performed relative to competitors across visibility, differentiation, and communication.

Even though this brand had decent shelf visibility, we had to confirm they effectively delivered across these facets, and the PPS confirmed it with clarity.

With this insight, the brand could refine its packaging strategy, not from scratch, but in a focused, data-backed way. Our work became a model for how we help brands navigate both product differentiation and shelf complexity.

MACHINE LEARNING POWERS PREDICTIVE INSIGHT

What exactly is machine learning?

Machine learning is a broad umbrella that spans a wide range of techniques. At one end are simple regression models, the kind many of us first encountered in high school math. On the more advanced end are convolutional neural networks (CNNs) and transformers, the latter of which power products like ChatGPT. Each of these approaches plays a role depending on the complexity of the data and the task at hand.

In our approach, we use a combination of regression models, CNNs, and transformers to train our systems through example, an approach known as *supervised machine learning*, the oldest and simplest way to train a model. We use it to make predictions on key behavioral metrics including claims, choices, and more. We do the following:

- Feed in data like images, survey results, real-world context, sales performance
- Show the model the actual results
- Let it learn patterns through exposure and feedback

The learning process is called *backward propagation*. The model makes a prediction, gets corrected, and then adjusts itself by re-weighting its internal connections.

This backward propagation approach, inherent to any neural network, allows the system to evolve with each new dataset, improving accuracy over time. The forward and backward propagation approaches are how a neural network "learns." The more examples it's given, the better it gets without needing to rewrite a single line of code. This is powerful in an insights-driven industry.

Machine learning is only as effective as the data, expertise, and structure behind it. That's why predictive models in packaging require 3 things: a deep, structured dataset; a team that understands both the technical and behavioral dimensions; and the right algorithms to connect them. Without these ingredients, even the most advanced models can fall short. All of these elements work together to give us a significant edge. Without a strong foundation of quality data, technical skill, and subject matter expertise, machine learning models can't deliver meaningful results. This trifecta of data, expertise, and modeling forms the foundation of any predictive system that aims to support real-world decision-making at scale.

INTERPRETING PACKS LIKE A SOMMELIER

If you're looking for a mental model to understand how our predictive engine works, particularly the role of AI systems, consider the sommelier.

A sommelier doesn't just taste wine. They interpret it. Using a combination of sensory inputs (sight, smell, taste), knowledge of regional classifications, grape varietals, and vintage nuances, they evaluate how well a wine meets expectations. They've tasted thousands of bottles, studied production methods, and learned what "good" should look, smell, and taste like across categories.

That's exactly what our predictive models do.

Like a sommelier, an AI system interprets multiple signals simultaneously: the visual hierarchy of a pack, its messaging and claims, its structural features, and its shelf context. It draws on an extensive behavioral database of millions of past interactions to recognize patterns and compare expectations to execution. It doesn't just see pixels or text. It understands meaning, context, and performance norms across product types and markets.

When a sommelier evaluates a 2008 Burgundy, they already know what it should taste like. They assess whether the wine meets the promise of its label. Our system does the same. When a shopper sees a new pack of premium granola, for example, our engine understands what cues shoppers expect from premium products in that category. Then, it evaluates whether the pack delivers.

This analogy isn't about romanticizing AI; it's about demystifying it. Like the sommelier, our system brings training, context, and real-world knowledge to bear. It doesn't guess; it evaluates, learns, and most importantly, helps us make confident decisions about what a pack will really do at shelf.

GENERATIVE VERSUS PREDICTIVE AI

Before we go any further (and as AI becomes more sophisticated), it's essential to distinguish between *generative AI* and *predictive AI*, as each serves a unique function in research. Both are powered by machine learning, but their applications in market research are fundamentally different.

- Generative AI is focused on creating new content. In the marketing world, it can generate ad copy, visuals, or even entirely new product concepts, but its role in packaging research is still developing. While it has the potential to assist with early-stage ideation, the real decision-making still requires grounded, behavioral data from actual consumers, which is where predictive AI plays a more critical role.
- Predictive AI is designed to forecast outcomes based on historical data. In packaging research, this means analyzing past shopper behavior to predict which designs will perform best in market. It identifies patterns, spots trends, and helps brands make data-driven decisions.

The book should make one point clear: Our AI is *predictive*, not generative. Its strength lies in using real shopper behavioral data to anticipate what works, not in generating speculative or hypothetical designs.

AI continues to evolve, opening up exciting possibilities for the future. Predictive models may soon be enhanced by generative elements by enabling products that not only forecast outcomes but also suggest smart packaging optimizations based on shopper engagement patterns. As these next-generation capabilities emerge, their impact will be strongest when built on the same rigorous, data-driven foundation that powers today's most trusted predictive insights.

Predictive AI has become the go-to in packaging research, helping brands refine designs before they hit the shelves, reduce risk, and base decisions on what truly drives shopper behavior, not just creative instinct. It's already transforming the way research is conducted: faster, more precise, and grounded in real-world data.

And this is only the beginning.

Imagine a future where AI doesn't just predict outcomes but helps teams iterate in real time, suggesting design optimizations based on how shoppers engage, guiding creative decisions before ideas even make it to testing. While we don't do that today, we're excited about the possibilities ahead. As technology evolves, we're building with the future in mind, open to integrating generative capabilities that enhance creative workflows.

Pitmaster LT's had a bold flavor story and a loyal regional following, but its packaging didn't communicate the brand's uniqueness. Shoppers were confused about the product, the value proposition wasn't clear, and shelf presence was getting lost in a crowded category.

We began by tapping into our world-leading behavioral database, allowing us to compare Pitmaster LT's designs against thousands of prior packaging tests. From there, we used Pack.AI (one of our AI-enabled products) to simulate performance across multiple routes by turning creative options into measurable data points that reflected real shopper behavior.

AI wasn't the star. It was the connective tissue, allowing us to rapidly scale testing and identify patterns that our database had already proven to drive attention, desire, and purchase.

Beyond packaging, we worked with Pitmaster LT's team to analyze their website performance and SEO visibility, ensuring that what worked on shelf could also translate to digital. We helped them develop a multichannel story, grounded in behavioral science and carried by consistent, compelling design.

By combining our behavioral science framework, structured database, and AI-powered modeling, Pitmaster LT's was able to:

- Clarify their visual equities and simplify communication
- Test multiple creative directions in parallel
- Translate pack improvements to e-commerce and SEO

The result: a faster path to shelf-ready design and a brand story that's clear, distinctive, and scalable across channels.[35]

OUR CORE INNOVATION: A SYSTEM THAT FORECASTS PACKAGING PERFORMANCE

At the heart of our most disruptive innovation is predictive AI, a transformative shift in how packaging research is done. We've built a system that forecasts packaging performance before it hits the shelf.

While AI isn't new to market research, its application at this level to predict shelf impact, purchase likelihood, and overall packaging sales effectiveness represents a true industry first.

Before we delve into our first 2 predictive AI products (PPS and Pack.AI), let's get into some of the details of our predictive platform and what unlocks the power of our proprietary dataset: computer vision AI and image analytics.

COMPUTER VISION AI AND IMAGE ANALYTICS

At the core of our predictive products is Computer Vision AI, which we apply using image analytics, a methodology that translates packaging visuals into structured, measurable data. Together, they allow us to evaluate packaging design the way a shopper does: quickly, instinctively, and contextually.

Computer vision AI simulates human visual processing, identifying and quantifying design elements such as:

- Brand marks: Logo size, placement, and visual dominance
- Color usage: Contrast, palette cohesion, and category differentiation
- Typography: Hierarchy, legibility, and communication efficiency
- Structure and shape: The role of pack format (size, shape relative to category commonalities, etc.)
- Claims and messaging: The presence, prominence, and clarity of claims analyzed in terms of language, context, and perceived impact (e.g., "Made in the USA" versus "USA Made")
- Brand stature: Recognition, established cues, and how the brand's perceived authority influences engagement
- Contextual indicators: Visual cues that suggest category leadership, shelf presence, or market familiarity (e.g., whether the brand is already well-known or established in market)
- Integrated design elements: How all components including text, imagery, claims, and layout work together to influence attention, trust, and purchase intent

Image analytics takes this further by contextualizing design execution within retail environments. It applies behavioral benchmarks from our database to assess how those visual elements impact actual shopper behavior like visibility at shelf, findability, and purchase.

PACK.AI AND PPS: FROM EXPERTISE TO PRODUCTIZATION

Pack.AI and PPS are, in many ways, the productization of our expertise. Over time, through consistent data collection, we've learned exactly what to capture and which KPIs actually move the needle on performance. These products automate the process, making it repeatable and scalable. They represent:

- A codification of our best practices
- An interface to our proprietary data
- A way to keep learning, predicting, and delivering value, again and again

By turning our expertise into products that can be leveraged in a systematic and repeatable way, we've created scalable products that continue to learn and improve. Pack.AI and PPS are built on a foundation of decades of experience and consistent data collection. Machine learning takes us further by uncovering patterns we could never have coded manually and delivering predictions with greater speed and precision.

By combining these 2 layers, what's on the pack and how it performs, we can quantify the effectiveness of every design decision. It's what makes our predictive AI products so powerful: They don't just analyze design; they predict how it will perform down to a single score or performance profile.

Now, let's get into the first of our predictive AI products: our PackPower Score.

WHAT IS THE PACKPOWER SCORE?

PackPower Score (PPS) is our proprietary predictive metric designed to assess the sales effectiveness of packaging. *It is seamlessly integrated into every product within the portfolio* and is the cornerstone of how we communicate value to our clients, especially those using multiple products across the suite.

At its core, the PPS is a single, easy-to-understand number that predicts the likely sales impact of a packaging design. It has been shown to *precisely predict* real-world outcomes, including that 5% sales increase following a packaging change that we mentioned in the beginning of the book.

The PPS isn't just a stand-alone score. It's backed by a behavioral framework that makes it actionable. Each PPS result is supported by a set of diagnostic drivers tied to the 4S framework. These 4 behavioral dimensions are further supported by granular KPIs that ladder up to the 4S scores, helping pinpoint exactly which elements are driving or hindering performance. This structure ensures that PPS not only predicts sales outcomes but also reveals the underlying *why* behind a pack's success or failure.

THE BENEFITS: WHY PPS MATTERS

PPS is the most critical metric because it reflects what matters most to our clients: sales impact. By distilling complex research findings into a single, predictive measure, PPS offers a clear benchmark for comparing current packaging designs against prospective ones or evaluating multiple new concepts in development. Its simplicity and clarity make it easy to interpret, while its scalability ensures consistency. Whether optimizing an existing design or launching a new product, PPS gives brands the confidence to make fast, informed decisions backed by behavioral data.

HOW PPS WORKS

PPS is built from 3 integrated components:

1. Computer Vision AI

Advanced AI models analyze pack designs in the way a human eye would, breaking down visual elements such as:

- Color schemes
- Structure and layout
- Key pack elements like brand marks, main visuals, text, and claims

These visual elements are converted into structured data that feeds into the model.

2. Survey Data/Database Data

We collect behavioral KPIs through studies simulating real-world shopping behavior. These always include but are not limited to:

- On-shelf metrics: Visibility, findability, and purchase
- Off-shelf metrics: Quality, brand efficacy, personal relevance, value, and trust

This is the additional dataset where Insights Analytics are applied—it's how consumers engage with packaging across contexts.

3. Sales Calibration

The final layer is real-world sales data, which is used to calibrate the model, ensuring that the prediction is tied to actual commercial outcomes. This grounds the PPS in what truly matters: driving sales transactions.

We've systematically connected billions of rows of second-party sales data to our own behavioral science database. That might sound simple, but it's an incredibly rare, hard-won capability.

This connection creates something truly unique: a longitudinal dataset that ties real-world shopper behavior directly to in-market outcomes. It's what allows us to predict sales impact with confidence, not just directionally, but quantitatively. The combination of our proprietary behavioral database and the systematic integration of sales performance gives our predictive engine its edge.

However, the real opportunity lies in what happens *after* launch. Because when behavioral drivers are connected to sales outcomes, the way we have done, brands can keep refining, optimizing and improving.

This is about staying competitive. Our system allows brands to continue learning post-launch, identifying what's working, what's not, and where the next gains can come from.

INTRODUCING: PACK.AI

Pack.AI is a predictive modeling product that uses computer vision AI and behavioral science frameworks to forecast packaging performance across multiple KPIs tied to driving transactions quickly, accurately, and at scale. Designed to support earlier-stage research and design development, Pack.AI empowers brands to test and iterate packaging designs *faster than ever before*, using real consumer data.

Built on the 4S framework (Be Seen, Be Shoppable, Be Seductive, and Be Selected), Pack.AI predicts how well a packaging design will perform across key behavioral KPIs that drive sales. Pack.AI is predictive modeling, trained on real shopper behavior to identify which packaging elements lead to marketplace success.

THE BENEFITS: WHY PACK.AI MATTERS

Pack.AI delivers at the speed of business, allowing our clients to test dozens or even hundreds of packaging designs rapidly. We've had clients test over 1,000 designs at a fraction of the time and cost of testing. It's well suited for early-stage development, enabling teams to create, iterate, and optimize designs well before committing to costly downstream production. Unlike products that rely solely on algorithmic projections, Pack.AI blends real human behavior with machine learning to deliver insights grounded in actual shopper responses. This means brands get predictive clarity early in the process, without sacrificing accuracy or depth.

Pack.AI also allows companies to model broad or narrow categories depending on business goals. For example, a beverage company could build a water-only model or expand to include enhanced waters and electrolyte drinks. The key is ensuring sensible inclusion of SKUs and consistency in measurement KPIs across the dataset. Pack.AI also enables flexible modeling by cycling in lower-share SKUs across multiple test versions for comprehensive category coverage.

We're not stopping at traditional retail. We're already applying Pack.AI in e-commerce environments, helping brands understand how packaging performs across digital platforms where visibility, messaging, and decision-making unfold differently than on physical shelves.

PACK.AI KEY USE CASES

Pack.AI supports 4 primary use cases across the entire packaging design life cycle.

1. In the creation and iteration phase, it allows teams to quickly evaluate a broad range of design directions using real behavioral data to guide early decision-making.
2. For competitive benchmarking, Pack.AI analyzes packaging alongside key competitors, offering insights that inform development and help sharpen your brand's positioning.
3. Once a promising design direction is identified, Pack.AI supports optimization, enabling brands to fine-tune details for maximum shopper impact before launch.
4. E-commerce performance: Pack.AI is already being applied to digital retail environments to measure how packs perform on virtual shelves, across devices, and within thumbnail views, helping brands adapt packaging for the unique demands of online shopping.

Together, these use cases demonstrate how Pack.AI brings speed, precision, and flexibility to every stage of the packaging journey whether on shelf or screen.

PACK.AI MODEL TYPES

Brands have flexibility in how they engage with Pack.AI, choosing between model types and additional modeling variables, based on their needs. Total Category Models are pre-built to cover broad product categories like beverages or food, enabling faster deployment and immediate insights. For more specialized needs, Custom Models offer a tailored approach, which is ideal for focused portfolios and specific client needs, e.g., not just food, not just snacks, not just salty snacks, but potato chips in specific regions and across specific shopper segments, providing needed relevance and precision.

INSIGHTS

Now, let's get back to the data science behind our products. How do we apply it? By testing brands whose packaging performance is already well-documented in our database. We use historical data on pack performance, behavioral metrics, and design characteristics to train our models to recognize patterns and predict outcomes.

CORRELATING VISUALS WITH OUTCOMES

Our models are trained to understand how specific pack images relate to performance outcomes. By processing large volumes of image data tied to real-world KPIs, the system learns these relationships over time. The result is a model that can take new input and predict performance based on what it's seen before. It does this through pattern recognition, learned correlations, and repeated exposure to visual elements tied to measurable outcomes.

MACHINES SEE MORE THAN WE DO

The model can process and interpret design elements at a level of detail that often surpasses human perception. It draws on contextual understanding from our database, including packaging structure, category norms, and design conventions. We also leverage technology that extracts and maps the visual hierarchy of each pack, identifying elements such as brand names, claims, and colors. This data is then enriched with insights from subject matter experts and additional sources to create a more complete and structured dataset. That structured data becomes the foundation Pack.AI uses to make predictions.

BUILT IN-HOUSE, SECURE BY DESIGN

We use some open-source software, but we don't rely on APIs or external AI platforms. We are not a wrapper around ChatGPT or any third-party generative tool. This matters for security and privacy. All our systems follow enterprise-grade compliance standards, including encryption at rest and in transit, multifactor authentication, and secured environments. When organizations use external APIs, they are subject to the data-handling policies of those platforms. In contrast, we built our products internally and operate under the same strict security protocols as the rest of our platform. Our clients' data stays protected, and our models are proprietary, built entirely by our in-house data science team.

PACK.AI'S ROLE IN THE CREATIVE FUNNEL

Exactly how do our database and AI work together? With Pack.AI.

Pack.AI enables rapid insight generation during early-stage design exploration. It allows teams to evaluate more concepts quickly, narrowing down what's most promising for deeper testing and validation. But we see its role expanding. Our vision is for Pack.AI to play a greater role in guiding the creative-design process, providing directional feedback on how to improve designs based on both qualitative and quantitative indicators.

ENHANCING CREATIVE WORKFLOWS

By using AI earlier in the workflow to power our database and make predictions, we are helping the brands we work with to reduce risk and optimize performance *before* reaching the validation stage. Instead of relying on limited testing or subjective evaluation, Pack.AI brings structured intelligence into the creative process. This enhances decision quality and confidence while allowing brand teams to explore more options with less friction.

PIXEL-LEVEL PRECISION, MULTIMODAL UNDERSTANDING

Pack.AI operates at a high level of granularity. It processes inputs at the pixel level, but also integrates multimodal data (text claims, visual elements, layout structure, and more). The system is able to handle a large number of variables, which are then synthesized into diagnostics that can be understood and used by marketers, designers, and insights teams.

HOW PPS DIFFERS FROM PACK.AI

So how is PPS different from Pack.AI? PPS is a prediction system that relies on our behavioral framework, the 4S's, and the integration of our sales data. That framework serves as our scorecard for strong pack design. If a design performs well, it tends to check most of those boxes. Within each "S," there are many KPIs that we either predict with products like Pack.AI or gather through survey-based methods.

The core challenge with PPS is connecting our behavioral database with market data. The answer? We build models that integrate behavioral performance with in-market results, models that can explain differences in sales performance.

We have an enormous volume of transaction data, tens of billions of data points linked to our behavioral database. This allows us to build models that can detect and explain shifts in market performance. For example, we can quantify when a product gains or loses share and map that back to design and behavioral metrics. If a pack experiences a 20% drop in market share or a 17% gain following a redesign, the model can isolate and explain those movements.

We're doing structured market research, controlled experiments with clear variables. These don't account for external disruptions like natural disasters or viral events, but they reflect the behavioral drivers that consistently influence shopper behavior.

PPS is a robust prediction product that can incorporate real-world contextual data. This includes more signals such as social media sentiment, brand reputation, and market noise so that our PPS models become even more robust and responsive to context.

Yes, our database can track trends and identify what has worked over time. And yes, human behavior in categories like health and beauty differs from food or pet care in ways that are deeply ingrained. But we also need to stay alert to how real-time brand context and cultural shifts affect performance.

That's the promise of machine learning. The technology keeps improving, and with it, our ability to incorporate more signals, more nuance, and more accuracy into the way we help brands make decisions.

Pack.AI and PPS are not just prediction products. They are part of a broader approach to creative enabling, empowering teams to iterate faster, reduce risk, and bring more effective packaging to market. That's how we bring our data science to life.

We've shown how this approach delivers powerful sales predictions grounded in shopper behavior. But what about broader strategic insights at the category level? Is there still room for that in a fast-moving, digital-first world?

Absolutely. We call it unPACKED.

UNPACKED: DELIVERING CATEGORY-LEVEL INSIGHTS

Think back to the very beginning of the book when we talked about chocolate. We opened with an unPACKED report to show you our robust dataset's offerings.

Our unPACKED reports aren't about prediction; they're about perspective. unPACKED is our syndicated product for brands that want a deeper understanding of how their category works and what it takes to win. Think of it as a strategic lens, not a forecasting product. Rather than tell you what will happen, unPACKED helps you see what is happening and why.

We start by collecting behavioral data the same way we do for our predictive models, using shopper-based evaluations in a controlled shelf environment. Then we analyze that data through the lens of the 4S's to uncover actionable, category-level insights.

The result? A clear, comparative view of the category landscape: which brands are winning and losing on shelf, what design elements drive performance, and where the opportunities lie to stand out and sell more.

As a bonus, because unPACKED follows the same rigorous data standards as our predictive work, the data can also be used to train future models. At its core though, unPACKED is about giving brands a strategic edge with clarity, not just calculation.

This comprehensive approach allows us to identify trends across multiple products within the same category whether it's chocolates, hair care, spirits, or any other segment. By understanding category-level patterns, brands gain a holistic view of what drives consumer choices within their specific market.

CATEGORY-LEVEL REPORTS

unPACKED reports provide a structured look at how packaging performs within specific product categories like beverages or skin care. Each report follows a consistent format, making it easy to compare across time or between segments.

These reports are designed to help brands make sense of what's really happening on the shelf. They show which packaging strategies are resonating with consumers, what visual cues are driving attention, and how specific design choices impact purchasing behavior.

Because each report is grounded in behavioral science, unPACKED breaks down how these behaviors play out in context.

For example, visibility is one of the most influential factors we measure, and our data shows that in many categories (including chocolate), products seen more often are approximately 2.5x more likely to be purchased.

These aren't abstract insights. We connect the dots between data and design, showing how real packages perform and highlighting the elements that set top performers apart. A beverage report, for instance, might explore how cues like condensation, color contrast, or bottle shape affect perceptions of refreshment or quality.

What sets unPACKED apart is its transparency. Users can trace insights directly back to the behavioral data behind them. This makes the findings not only informative but usable, clear enough to spark strategy, concrete enough to support design decisions.

TRANSFORMING PACKAGING RESEARCH AND WHAT COMES NEXT

Throughout this chapter, we've shown how predictive AI has transformed packaging research from weeks-long studies to real-time, behaviorally grounded predictions. With products like PPS and Pack.AI, brands can test, iterate, and optimize packaging at scale faster, cheaper, and more accurately than ever before. These innovations deliver more than just efficiency; they provide confident, data-backed decisions grounded in what consumers actually do, not just what they say.

But speed and scale are only part of the story.

One of the most underappreciated strengths of our approach is that it doesn't rely solely on automation. While predictive AI powers rapid iteration and measurable performance, our work is also grounded in rigorous human analysis.

Emma, Marisol, and Steven could all gain from the speed, scale, and precision offered by predictive tools. For Emma, iterative testing with Pack.AI could help her explore bolder creative routes with less risk and faster feedback, allowing her to evolve a heritage brand without alienating its core. Marisol, as she navigates a fast-paced category and tight timelines, could use predictive modeling to compare design options in real time, ensuring her team's gut instincts are backed by scalable data. And Steven, working across a global organization with varied regional needs, could rely on AI-calibrated KPIs and benchmarked results to unify internal stakeholders. These products aren't just efficient. They're flexible, adaptive, and built to keep pace with today's most complex packaging challenges.

This chapter was about the power of our products and how they deliver speed, scale, and value. Next is about how these products will help predict ambiguous consumers.

Let's unPACK it.

TL;DR: Delivering Speed, Scale, and Value

- Challenge: In fast-paced markets, brands needed a way to test more designs, iterate quickly, and make confident decisions backed by data—not by instinct.
- Traditional Limitations: In-person studies often took months and were limited in scale and scope. Digital solutions helped but still struggled to bridge the gap between speed and rigor.
- Our Solution: We introduced predictive AI into packaging research through productized tools like Pack.AI and PPS. Built on our behavioral science framework and trained on the largest packaging database in the world, these products simulate real-world behavior, predict performance outcomes, and deliver results in minutes, not weeks. With pixel-level analysis and category-specific modeling, we help brands predict how packaging will perform at shelf and online with speed, accuracy, and context.
  - Key Benefits:
    - Instant evaluation of early-stage designs across the 4S framework
    - Predictive modeling trained on hundreds of millions of real shopper interactions
    - Products that quantify visual performance and forecast sales impact
    - Flexible model types that adapt to e-commerce, regional nuances, or niche segments
    - Integration of computer vision, behavioral diagnostics, and sales calibration
- Impact: Colgate used Pack.AI to identify a high-performing design for its Total Plaque Pro Release toothpaste, achieving standout shelf presence and winning *Allure*'s "Best of Beauty" award. A major coffee creamer brand clarified its value prop-

osition using PPS to benchmark pack communication in a crowded category. Pitmaster LT's scaled testing with Pack.AI, optimized both shelf and digital presence, and aligned their story across touchpoints. These successes show how predictive AI enables smarter, faster, and more scalable design decisions.

Chapter 7.

PREDICTING AMBIGUOUS CONSUMERS

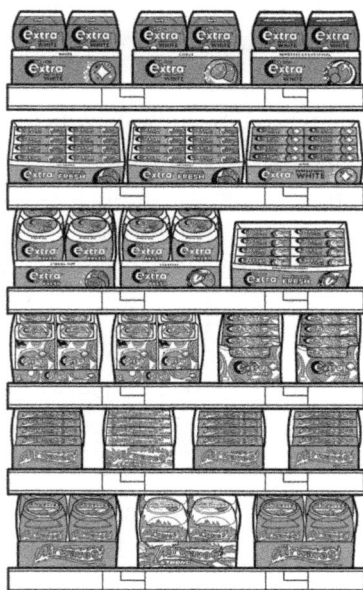

Mars Wrigley set out to refresh the visual identity of 4 of its flagship chewing gum brands: Orbit, Extra, Freedent, and Yida. With a growing global footprint and evolving consumer expectations, the goal was clear: determine which new design would perform best on shelf across multiple markets. The challenge wasn't just about aesthetics; it was about identifying a packaging system that would stand out, drive purchase, and clearly communicate freshness across geographies.

To guide this complex redesign, Mars Wrigley leveraged our predictive behavioral research products to evaluate performance across countries. The study included:

- PackFlash, a digitally simulated shelf-testing environment, to evaluate shopper behavior in context
- Testing conducted across 4 global markets, ensuring cultural relevance and international applicability
- Behavioral KPIs focused on visibility, communication clarity, navigation efficiency, and purchase conversion

This helped Mars Wrigley quantify which design elements performed best and isolate the visual systems that would deliver consistency and impact across global shelves.

The behavioral testing revealed a clear winner: a design that delivered enhanced visibility and drove stronger purchase interest. We found:

- Clear improvements in shopper navigation and visual hierarchy
- Stronger performance for visual cues tied to freshness
- Specific design refinements recommended such as enhancing the prominence of the "leaf" visual to further emphasize freshness perception

The predictive results gave Mars Wrigley high confidence in the selected direction. The combination of shopper-based testing and clear behavioral data led to cross-functional alignment and faster decision-making. With a new global design informed by shopper behavior and validated across regions, Mars Wrigley is now positioned to launch a unified visual identity that connects across cultures and sells at shelf.[36]

A PERPLEXING PACKAGING CHALLENGE

Emma, introduced to you earlier in the book, is an experienced brand leader tasked with a deceptively difficult challenge: redesigning the packaging for a beloved heritage snack. For decades, the brand had enjoyed unwavering loyalty from older shoppers who knew what they liked and stuck with it. But today, the numbers told a different story. Sales were declining, and younger consumers weren't buying. They walked past the product without so much as a second glance, their attention captured by cleaner, more modern packs that looked nothing like Emma's established brand.

Her team responded with a bold redesign: a stripped-down logo, a contemporary color palette, and a more modern structure. The response? A mix of confusion, hesitation, and frustration. Long-time shoppers felt disoriented. New ones didn't recognize the product or what it stood for. What should have been a clear solution became a cautionary tale.

At the center of this dilemma were the ambiguous consumers, the ones who say they want heritage but choose what's new and shiny, who crave trust but are seduced by novelty. They research online, shop across channels, and demand both familiarity and change often in the same breath.

Emma wasn't just designing for 2 audiences. She was designing for 1 audience split down the middle. And with every iteration, she felt the stakes rise. Shift too far toward modern, and she'd lose her loyal base. Stay too close to tradition, and she'd miss the new wave entirely.

What she needed wasn't just inspiration, it was insight. A way to understand what both sides of her audience do, not just what they say.

Now, she has it.

We will show you how brands can confidently navigate one of the most perplexing packaging challenges today: ambiguous consumers.

These are the shoppers who defy simple segmentation: They want tradition and innovation, simplicity and substance, trust and disruption. You'll revisit Emma's brand story and see how predictive analytics and behavioral diagnostics helped her team design with dual audiences in mind, by bringing clarity to contradiction and helping them understand what drives choice without relying solely on what consumers claim to want. Along the way, you'll see how behavioral science gives teams the insight and alignment they need to confidently redesign for a fragmented, fast-moving market.

CAPRI SUN AND THE PUBLIC BACKLASH

Capri Sun's recent packaging innovation highlights the complexities brands face when appealing to "ambiguous consumers," those who desire both nostalgia and modern convenience. In 2024, the brand introduced 12-ounce resealable bottles to cater to adults seeking a more portable option. This move aimed to expand Capri Sun's presence in convenience stores and accommodate on-the-go lifestyles.

However, the change sparked significant backlash from long-time fans who cherished the iconic pouch-and-straw experience. Social media erupted with comments mourning the perceived loss of a childhood staple, with some declaring it "one of the most shocking product changes in history." Capri Sun responded by clarifying that the pouches would remain available.[37]

Packaging changes can resonate deeply, influencing not just purchasing decisions but brand perception as a whole.

AMBIGUOUS CONSUMERS AND THE PACKAGING PROBLEM

Ambiguous consumers are rewriting the rules of packaging. These aren't neatly defined personas or predictable demographic groups. They blur lines between age brackets, between value systems, and between shopping modes. One week, they want the lowest price; the next, they're impulse-buying premium wellness snacks. They crave newness but default to what's familiar. They scroll endlessly for inspiration, then walk into the store and buy the same thing they always do.

This shape-shifting behavior makes packaging harder than ever before to get right. Brands can no longer rely on generalizations like the idea that younger shoppers prefer minimalist design, or that older consumers are loyal to only established aesthetics. Ambiguous consumers don't play by those rules. They want it all. And if a pack doesn't offer multiple levels of appeal, if it can't communicate freshness and familiarity, or disruption and trust, shoppers will move on without hesitation.

Designing for these shoppers isn't about walking a tightrope. It's about navigating a moving target. And to do that, brands need more than intuition—they need evidence. Products that tell you what looks good, *and* what works across fragmented, contradictory audiences.

WHY BEHAVIORAL SCIENCE IS ESSENTIAL FOR AMBIGUOUS CONSUMERS

Like we've discussed at length, one of the biggest challenges with ambiguous consumers is the gap between what they say they want and what they do. This isn't a new phenomenon but it's growing more acute as today's shoppers engage with a greater number of brands, across more channels, more frequently, and with higher expectations for personalization and relevance.

As we know, Dooley and Fogg have both spoken directly to this tension. For ambiguous consumers—those who toggle between categories, behaviors, and preferences—this contradiction is especially pronounced. They may say they want something familiar and heritage driven but then walk out of the store with a minimalist, design-forward pack. Or they may tell a survey they prefer clean labels, then gravitate toward the most indulgent option on the shelf.

This is why our approach is grounded in observation. As Dooley explains, the key is observing decision-making "in full context," ensuring that what we're seeing reflects how real people act in real moments of choice. Rather than relying solely on self-reported data, we capture real behavior, how shoppers navigate the aisle or scroll the digital shelf, what they notice, and what they choose.

PackFlash, Pack.AI, PPS, and unPACKED were all built on this principle. They move beyond claimed preferences to model behavior dynamically. They simulate both the decision context (in-store and online) and the decision-makers (loyalists, trend-seekers, or new adopters). And they allow teams to test, iterate, and refine in scalable, repeatable ways ensuring that ambiguous audiences are being met with evidence.

For brands like Emma's, this behavioral foundation is crucial. It means they're not just following what consumers say they want. They're designing based on what moves them to act.

FROM MACRO TO CRAFT TO
SELTZER: MATT'S STORY

I've always found beer to be one of the clearest examples of how consumer preferences evolve and how categories respond. For example, it used to be all about macro brews. In the past, you could grab a 30-pack of Budweiser, Coors, or Miller for cheap, and it was all about volume for your dollar.

But then something shifted. Consumers got curious about flavor, quality, and ingredients. Enter craft beer. First it was pale ales, then IPAs exploded with big, bold, hoppy brews that became the new standard for cool. I remember when sours had their moment, and suddenly every taproom was offering one. But the pendulum kept swinging. High ABV wasn't sustainable for everyday drinking, and people started looking for something lighter.

That's when the "day drinking" beers took off, like Founders' All Day IPA or Lagunitas DayTime. Low alcohol, full flavor. It was a smarter indulgence. And then, just like that, the door opened to a whole new category: hard seltzers. Suddenly, it wasn't even about beer anymore. It was about refreshment: something crisp, easy to drink, and not too filling. Mixed cocktails in a can followed right behind.

To me, it was a perfect storm of evolving tastes, cultural shifts, and category reinvention. Watching that progression from macro to craft to seltzer was like seeing the entire industry learn, pivot, and keep innovating to meet the moment and meet the consumers where they were.

THE NEED FOR DECISION PRECISION

For Emma, the stakes were high. Redesigning a beloved established pack meant walking a razor's edge; one wrong move could confuse loyal customers, while hesitation could cost her the next generation of buyers. She didn't just need inspiration; she needed decision precision.

STEP 1: DIAGNOSE

Emma starts by establishing what her product communicates, through both research and how the packaging influences brand and product perceptions.

The goal is to define design guardrails that keep her close enough to existing equity without limiting the brand's ability to evolve. She is looking for a sweet spot: not straying too far from what worked today but adapting where needed, especially with the introduction of new SKUs.

That could mean unifying elements across the portfolio or figuring out which design cues from the current packaging need to be carried over as is and where there is creative latitude to draw in new shoppers.

She wants to understand what her packaging commonly communicates so she can ensure the design delivers on the category's core expectations both visually and behaviorally.

Emma also needs to know how to attract *new* customers; she needs to see how her brand stacks up against its competitors. Is her brand visible at the level of best-in-class competitors? Is it easily found at shelf?

Ultimately, she needs to learn how both her current and potential new packaging aligns with the signals coming from the rest of the category. She then must identify what to continue to communicate clearly, like quality or relevance, to stay competitive with existing customers *and* capture new shoppers.

When Emma tells us her packaging research goals, and the challenges she faces with the snack brand's ambiguous consumers, we suggest she take a look at the unPACKED report for her category: salty snacks. We tell her it will answer all her questions, so she can thoroughly research how consumers relate with her brand and how it performs against its competitors.

Emma reviews the unPACKED report for salty snacks and finds a clear picture of how shoppers respond to the brand. She sees what longtime customers value about the original packaging and where there may be room for thoughtful updates.

From there, Emma turns those insights into a design brief.

STEP 2: BUILD A STRATEGY BASED ON REAL INSIGHTS

unPACKED: Salty Snacks Report identifies how Emma's heritage snack brand performs today, the areas it needs to compete in to meet category expectations (the cost of entry), and where the white space opportunities lie: spaces the brand can uniquely own. For example, if the opportunity is to communicate "healthier" or highlight an ingredient like "coconut oil," those become strategic priorities for design.

Emma takes everything she's learned from unPACKED, defines a strategy, and brings it to her design team, where she shares clear objectives for the next phase:

1. Use design elements that maintain the brand's current strengths, particularly quality and relevance in the market.
2. Don't veer too far from the existing background color, since that visual equity helps build a recognizable brand block and supports visibility.
3. Capitalize on the identified opportunity like positioning the product as a better-for-you (BFY) chip made with coconut oil. That signal should come through visually whenever possible, but also through supporting copy.

Using insights from unPACKED, Emma gives the design team clear, evidence-based direction grounded in behavioral insight.

STEP 3: EXPLORE AND TEST WITH PACK.AI

Once Emma's design team has developed a range of new packaging routes, the next step is testing. Using Pack.AI, the team evaluates each design against behavioral KPIs, identifying which options perform best and which fall short. The weaker designs are eliminated, while the stronger ones are refined further.

Let's say Designs A1 and X1 outperform the rest. The team then builds on those directions, generating iterations like A2, A3, A4 and X2, X3, X4 with each informed by behavioral feedback. With each round, the designs get sharper, more targeted, and better aligned with the brand's strategic objectives.

As testing continues, the team ensures each design direction continues to deliver on the foundational pillars of quality and relevance. Whether it's a redesign or a new line extension, the new packs must convey the same signals that made the original product trusted and beloved. Even if the format shifts, the underlying perception must remain strong—especially for existing loyalists.

In the past, testing 5 design routes might have taken a month. Now, with Pack.AI, Emma's team can test tens, even hundreds, of designs in moments, exploring a wide creative territory without sacrificing speed or rigor. What once took a month can now be accomplished in a matter of days, with data guiding every iteration.

Even better, Pack.AI allows Emma to tailor her testing strategy to specific goals like maintaining loyalty among existing consumers while attracting new shoppers. With advanced modeling capabilities, the team can even test how different designs resonate with brand users, nonusers, and competitive brand users. That means Emma can confidently zero in on the pack that's most likely to win at shelf across all priority audiences.

STEP 4: VALIDATE WITH PACKFLASH

Emma has narrowed the field to 2 final design routes. Predictive modeling gave her a strong signal, but she also needed reassurance that real shoppers would respond to the new pack the way the models suggested. After all, as a brand leader, the last place she wanted to be was sitting in front of the CEO, defending a major redesign that had never been shown to consumers.

So she turned to PackFlash, Behaviorally's digitally simulated shelf-testing environment, as a final validation step.

PackFlash placed the new pack in context on a crowded virtual shelf surrounded by competitors and captured real-time shopper behavior. Emma could see whether her design was being noticed, if shoppers could navigate to it easily, and how it performed on key metrics like purchase intent and communication clarity.

The results gave her what predictive models alone couldn't: external validation and internal confidence. With clear behavioral data from real consumers, Emma could walk into executive meetings and creative reviews with a grounded story, one that combined the realism of consumer testing with the precision of predictive AI.

STEP 5: PREDICT PERFORMANCE WITH PPS

Once she validated performance with real shoppers, Emma needed a clear, quantified signal to guide her final decision. That's where the PackPower Score (PPS) came in.

With PPS, she gained a single predictive benchmark that told her which of her 2 validated designs was most likely to drive incremental sales in market.

For her redesign, PPS could anchor its predictions to the current benchmark, providing a clear view of which route was most likely to improve commercial performance. That made PPS especially valuable: It didn't just tell Emma which design was visually strong. It told her which was expected to sell better.

For a redesign like Emma's, PPS offered something critical: decision precision. With one number, her team could see which design delivered the greatest sales impact.

The results gave her what predictive models alone couldn't: external validation and internal confidence. Now, with clear behavioral data from real consumers, Emma could walk into executive meetings and creative reviews with a grounded story, one that combined the precision of AI with the realism of consumer testing.

TOM'S OF MAINE: DESIGNING FOR MODERN APPEAL

Before   After

Tom's of Maine began a redesign journey to modernize its deodorant packaging and expand its appeal across gender lines in a traditionally gendered category. The brand needed a fresh structural and visual system that would resonate with evolving consumer expectations around simplicity, sustainability, and natural ingredients.

We began by conducting visual equity research to identify the pack elements most essential to brand recognition and appeal. From there, our team applied a multimodal methodology leveraging qualitative, quantitative, and AI-powered tools to explore design routes and optimize for shelf navigation and clarity of desired messaging. Iterative testing allowed for continuous refinement, leading to a winning pack design backed by data.

The final optimized design delivered across key behavioral metrics:

- 84% of Tom's buyers were able to correctly find the deodorant at shelf (versus 75% for the 2023 design)
- 71% perceived the products as made with natural ingredients (versus 59% in 2023)
- 42% of category shoppers viewed Tom's as a sustainable brand (versus 28% in 2023)

With the right insights, established brands can evolve without alienating loyal consumers. The redesign helped Tom's of Maine modernize its image while deepening associations with sustainability and naturalness, strengthening relevance in a shifting market.[38]

THE NEW REALITY OF PACKAGING DESIGN

Ambiguity among consumers isn't a passing phase; it's core to who they are (System 1 Thinking) and exacerbated by a retail environment that's more dynamic, layered, and expectation-driven than ever before. Ambiguous consumers reflect a broader shift in how people shop: by context, mood, and intent. For brands like

Emma's, succeeding with these consumers means mastering the art of duality, serving multiple needs without diluting the brand, modernizing without alienating, and evolving without losing what made the product beloved in the first place.

And with predictive analytics and behavioral diagnostics, she can test designs quickly, predict sales accurately, and finally validate with consumers, too. Decision precision at its finest.

The gamble is gone. In its place: data-backed clarity, strategic alignment, and precise packaging that resonates with the very people who once seemed impossible to pin down.

TL;DR: Predicting Ambiguous Consumers

- Challenge: Ambiguous consumers are hard to pin down—they want both innovation and tradition, modernity and familiarity. This makes packaging redesign risky and complex.

- Traditional Limitation: Ambiguity leads to upstream design work, and brands simply don't have the budget to test multiple designs across specific audience segments.

- Our Solution: We use behavioral diagnostics and predictive products—unPACKED, Pack.AI, PackFlash, and PPS—to simulate real shelf conditions, benchmark against category norms, and deliver fast, data-driven insights that help brands confidently navigate complex, fragmented audiences.

  ◦ Key Benefits:

    · unPACKED identifies which design cues resonate with both loyalists and new adopters by benchmarking current packaging against category norms and shopper behavior.

    · Pack.AI enables fast iteration of dozens of early-stage designs, revealing what works for different segments, without blowing the budget or slowing down development.

    · PackFlash validates final design routes in realistic shelf environments, ensuring consumer response matches predictions before going to market.

    · PPS quantifies expected sales impact and anchors design decisions in predictive, commercial outcomes.

    · The suite enables cross-functional alignment between insights, design, and executive teams by translating behavioral ambiguity into data-backed clarity.

- Impact: Mars Wrigley used predictive testing across multiple markets to identify a globally resonant pack for its gum portfolio. Tom's of Maine redesigned its deodorant with cross-gender appeal and boosted perceptions of naturalness and sustainability. Emma used our suite of products, from unPACKED to PPS, to redesign a heritage snack brand, balancing equity and innovation with precision.

Chapter 8.

LEVEL THE PLAYING FIELD

Before

After

Soupergirl, a purpose-driven soup brand built on fresh ingredients and social values, had a growing retail footprint, but their packaging wasn't keeping pace. Despite loyal customers and strong brand principles, Soupergirl's existing pack architecture didn't clearly communicate the product benefits or brand story. Shopper research revealed key barriers: Consumers weren't noticing the product on shelf, weren't clear on the value proposition, and weren't compelled to act. Soupergirl hoped to revamp their packaging to stand out, unify the portfolio, and drive both clarity and conversion at retail.

To meet Soupergirl's needs for deep insight, fast iteration, and confident prediction, our team deployed a custom research program leveraging 3 key products:

- Pack.AI to vet the pack's potential across a wide range of design elements, visual cues, and communication patterns using AI-trained models built on real behavioral data
- PackFlash to evaluate the current and proposed packaging in realistic, behavioral shelf contexts, assessing what consumers noticed, understood, and chose
- PackPower Score (PPS) to quantify the predicted sales impact of each design and benchmark them against normative data
- This trio provided diagnostic insight and a quantified prediction of market impact

The test design significantly outperformed the original across key behavioral dimensions:

- Be Seductive: Communication of "good source of protein" improved from 26% to 39%; "worth paying more" rose from 22% to 36%
- Be Selected: Purchase from shelf increased from 20% to 29%
- PPS: Predicted a +2.5% sales lift based on design performance

Our prediction was conservative. After launching the new pack design, Soupergirl saw a 5% lift in sales, driven by stronger shelf presence, clearer communication, and a more compelling brand story. The updated packaging resonated with shoppers and unlocked new retail channels for the brand.[39]

HOW RETAIL COMPLEXITY AFFECTS PACKAGING

Packaging innovation is critical because the modern retail landscape is a consumer-attention labyrinth. With countless products vying for space on digital and physical shelves, small brands face an uphill battle to differentiate themselves, capture interest, and drive conversions. In an era when consumers are bombarded with choices, packaging plays a critical role in breaking through the noise.

But the challenge isn't just about standing out; it's about standing out in the right way, at the right time, and in the right place. Packaging effectiveness is shaped by 4 key retail complexities:

- The Sea of Sameness
- Choice Overload
- Retailer-Specific Merchandising
- Shelf Competition

Each has implications for brand strategy.

To address the first major challenge in retail, we must consider the Sea of Sameness, a phenomenon where category conventions blur brand identities. Let's explore why standing out visually is crucial for capturing consumer attention.

THE SEA OF SAMENESS

One of the biggest challenges brands face today is visual clutter, with many product categories having become overwhelmingly similar in design, color schemes, and messaging. This phenomenon, what we like to refer to as the Sea of Sameness, makes it difficult for consumers to quickly distinguish one brand from another.

Take a walk down the personal care, beverage, or snack aisle and you'll notice the problem firsthand.

Competing brands mimic category norms, often leading to indistinguishable designs that blur together on the shelf. While category conventions are important for establishing familiarity, too much uniformity leads to brand invisibility.

To win in these environments, brands must find ways to balance category recognition with distinctiveness by leveraging color, structure, typography, and iconography to create a unique visual identity without alienating consumers.

CHOICE OVERLOAD

Consumers today have more product options than ever before. While variety can be a selling point, too much choice can lead to decision fatigue, where overwhelmed shoppers either default to familiar brands, delay purchase decisions, or abandon the purchase altogether.

Grocery aisles, e-commerce pages, and even convenience store shelves are packed with variations including multiple sizes, flavors, formulations, and packaging formats all competing for attention. While these options provide consumers with more choices, they also increase cognitive load, making it harder for them to make quick, confident purchase decisions.

Effective packaging cuts through the clutter by making the decision-making process easier. Strong visual cues, clear product benefits, and intuitive design help shoppers quickly identify the best choice for their needs, reducing friction at the moment of purchase. This is where behavioral science plays a critical role. Fogg's Behavior Model reminds us that a behavior happens when motivation, ability, and a prompt all converge, meaning even a motivated shopper can abandon a purchase if a pack is hard to understand or lacks a clear call to action. Dooley's work on cognitive fluency further reinforces this: When something feels easier to process, it's more likely to be trusted and chosen. In crowded retail environments, the most effective packaging reduces mental effort by clearly signaling key benefits and guiding shoppers effortlessly toward a decision. This isn't just good design, it's applied behavioral science that aligns with how people actually shop.

RETAILER-SPECIFIC MERCHANDISING

Not all products are displayed the same way across retailers. Mass merchandisers, grocery stores, convenience stores, and pharmacies each have unique layouts, category flows, and point-of-sale materials. From vertical versus horizontal shelving to how SKUs and brands are grouped, every environment introduces subtle differences that can influence shopper behavior and packaging performance.

It's become even more challenging in retail environments where products are increasingly placed behind lock and key, creating additional barriers for shoppers and impacting impulse purchases.[40]

Merchandising strategies vary significantly—there are possibilities to run products by brand, flavor, price point, or usage occasion. Mass beverage retailers, for example, may prioritize price-point-driven placement, requiring brands to emphasize value cues more prominently. This inconsistency creates a major challenge for packaging effectiveness.

Because brands can influence but can't control how products are shelved, packaging must be designed to stand out in multiple display scenarios. This means ensuring that key elements such as brand name, benefits, and product differentiators are immediately visible from multiple angles and distances.

SHELF COMPETITION: FIGHTING FOR PRIME REAL ESTATE AND VISIBILITY

Shelf placement is one of the most influential factors in purchase decisions, but not all shelf space is created equal. Retailers often give prime real estate to brands that are category leaders, exclusive partnerships, or private labels, making it even harder for smaller or emerging brands to compete. Shelf space is incredibly valuable real estate, and for a new brand trying to break in, it's nearly impossible without serious financial backing.[41]

The most effective packaging strategies take the following into account:

- Eye-level versus bottom-shelf placement: Products at eye level get far more visibility than those placed elsewhere, and bottom shelves are often overlooked. Our unPACKED category reports reveal that across the vast majority of categories, brands seen most are bought at least 2.5x more than those seen least on average.
- Crowding from competitors: Packaging must drive instant recognition even when surrounded by similar products.
- Impulse versus planned purchases: Packaging for impulse-driven products (e.g., snacks, beverages) must be attention-grabbing, while packaging for planned purchases (e.g., skin care, household essentials) must reinforce trust and reliability.

With so many brands competing for the same limited space, packaging must do more than just look good. It must command attention, clearly communicate its value, and drive consumer action in mere seconds. Shopping is facilitated with quick and clear packaging communication—our database reveals that the fastest-found designs (top 25% of fastest found) increase accuracy of finding levels by 20 percentage points compared to those in the bottom 25%—proving that frustration can lead to choosing something unintended.

CAN NEW AND SMALL BRANDS COMPETE?

In this hypercompetitive environment, where prime shelf space is scarce and visual noise is constant, even the most well-formulated products can get overlooked. And while established brands have the budget and buyer leverage to maintain visibility, smaller players often get crowded out both physically and psychologically.

So how can new and small brands compete?

You remember Marisol. She's the manager of a small, mission-driven vitamin brand that is elegantly designed, ethically sourced, and virtually invisible. Her minimalist packaging, crafted to reflect sustainability and wellness, was getting buried on shelf and lost online. Her few loyal customers loved the product, but everyone else? They never even saw it.

Marisol's challenge wasn't her formula; it was her visibility. Competing against neon-colored giants and consistently optimized rivals, she was up against a complex retail environment that demanded different strategies for physical and digital shelves. She didn't just need a good product. She needed to be seen, understood, and chosen everywhere her consumers shopped.

That's the reality brands face today: crowded store aisles, endless scrolls of thumbnails, and shopper expectations that shift depending on the channel. And for smaller brands like Marisol's, the margin for error is razor thin. She has a very, very small research budget.

But what if Marisol had research that allowed her to gain insights into her brand's category and test as many designs as she wanted within that budget?

Would this help her solve her challenges of breaking through at shelf as a new brand in a complex retail environment?

BE CHOSEN AT SHELF

Reaching new or underserved audiences isn't just about media targeting or product innovation, but about being seen, understood, and chosen at shelf. In a crowded and competitive landscape, the right packaging doesn't just draw attention; it speaks to the people you're trying to reach.

SEEING IS SELLING: BENCHMARKING REAL VISIBILITY

At the most fundamental level, a shopper has to see your product to buy it. That sounds obvious, but in practice, many brands underestimate how hard it is to earn visibility on shelf especially if you're a newer or smaller player. Through our engine, we can help new and small brands, too. Our unPACKED reports are accessible to all brands, regardless of age or size.

What does that mean for Marisol? She can use unPACKED to do a temperature check on her category: vitamins. She can review visibility benchmarks so she can develop a design strategy to get her new brand seen at shelf and selected for purchase.

Marisol now has a clear picture of what "good enough" looks like in her category, so she can determine how her brand can outperform. This knowledge helps her and her design teams understand how shelf placement, pack orientation, and design all affect whether consumers even notice the product, an essential insight for brands looking to reach new audiences who aren't already familiar with them.

LEARNING WHAT WORKS AND FOR WHOM

Once Marisol's product is visible, it has to connect. And that connection varies depending on the audience she's trying to reach.

unPACKED breaks down the design tactics that work across different product types and shopper needs. For Marisol, who is trying to reach a new type of shopper, this insight is gold. It helps her speak the visual language her desired audience understands. unPACKED is based on data critical to driving transactions and leverages expert interpretation. It's a predictive, human-diagnostic product.

FINDING THE GAPS THAT OTHERS MISS

This diagnostic product isn't only for new and small brands; it can be used for any brand, including niche brands.

Rather than rely on assumptions, unPACKED shows brands how the category is behaving. Where are the design redundancies? Which pack structures dominate? What claims are underused but gaining traction? These are the types of patterns that surface when we zoom out and examine the category through a behavioral lens.

For brands entering a new segment, this becomes a strategic playbook. They can see where competitors are clustering and where the white space lives. And because the data is grounded in what shoppers do (not just what they say), the insights are highly actionable.

NAVIGATING THE POWER DYNAMICS OF SHELF REAL ESTATE

Marisol knows firsthand that not every brand has the luxury of centralized shelf placement or large brand blocks. For emerging brands, success often depends on knowing how to play smart within a limited footprint.

unPACKED helps Marisol decode the competitive dynamics at shelf: who's dominating, what they're doing well, and how other brands can work around them.

She can use all of this information to influence design routes.

This isn't just about emulating the leaders. It's about developing pragmatic, design-forward strategies that help newer entrants make an outsized impact with the space they do have. Whether it's maximizing contrast, using disruptive pack structures, or homing in on a differentiated value proposition, our category-level reporting helps translate shelf realities into smart design decisions.

Ultimately, Marisol walks away with a concrete, research-backed design strategy, one that respects what's working in the category but breaks free of its blind spots. And for a small brand with a limited budget, that kind of clarity is a game changer.

THE IMPACT OF SEASONAL PACKAGING: MATT'S STORY

Kleenex has consistently demonstrated how subtle packaging changes can drive incremental growth. One particularly effective tactic has been their use of seasonal box designs by rotating color palettes and patterns to align with winter, spring, summer, and fall.

What might appear to be a simple design change actually delivers a powerful behavioral nudge. These seasonal visuals resonate with consumers' environments and moods, often leading to repeat or additional purchases. People begin choosing boxes not just for function, but to complement their home or reflect the time of year.

Kleenex doesn't need to reinvent the product. They just adapt the story of the packaging.

Packaging that evolves seasonally can maintain brand relevance and drive purchase frequency, especially when it connects to emotional cues like time of year, home aesthetics, or personal expression.

USING PREDICTIVE DESIGN TESTING TO GAIN CLARITY

Once Marisol has a strategic direction for her packaging, the next step is turning those insights into tangible design concepts. With limited budget and time, she can't afford to rely on guesses or wait weeks to evaluate just a handful of options.

Instead, she uses Pack.AI to test dozens of early-stage designs at once, quickly identifying which variations perform best across key behavioral metrics: visibility, shoppability, desirability, and purchase intent. Her team learns not just which designs look good, but which are most likely to succeed with real shoppers both online and in store.

One of the most powerful advantages? She can test against niche audiences, like plant-based wellness shoppers, without overspending. Normally, fielding with low-incidence groups is expensive and inefficient. But here, once behavioral data has been collected, it can be reused, which allows Marisol to model performance for future designs without needing to re-recruit or re-field.

She moves faster, spends smarter, and makes confident creative decisions grounded in real consumer behavior.

This flexibility allows brands to test far more designs than previously possible while still targeting exactly the right audience. The result is faster learning, smarter iteration, and ultimately an improved design.

LIMITED TIME OFFERS (LTOS)

When brands launch limited time offers (LTOs), like packs with promotions for the Super Bowl or Olympics, timing is everything. Ideally, testing takes place during the according time frame to accurately capture behaviors during the real-time moment. But once the moment passes, it is difficult to capture behaviors truly reflective of the season (in this example). Pack.AI captures real shopper behavior in the moment, and the behavioral data from one LTO campaign can be remodeled and applied to future explorations, even if not in the real-time moment. Instead of starting from scratch or guessing what might work, teams can use the learning from the actual point-in-time to test and refine new concepts with data reflecting the true time period. That means sharper creative direction, better-informed decisions, and less time and money spent revalidating what the team already knows.

SEASONAL VARIANTS

Wouldn't it be great if capturing seasonal, timely sentiment was a little easier?

Seasonal products, such as Halloween or Valentine's Day themed items (Cadbury eggs come to mind for Easter), require research conducted during the relevant time frame to accurately capture consumer sentiment. In the past, brands often skipped testing these designs altogether because they didn't have the time or money. With our products, those limitations are gone. Our products allow brands to evaluate seasonal packaging efficiently and effectively by leveraging historical shopper data and testing early-stage designs. (unPACKED can also help with seasonal variants to decode the drivers of past seasonal success.)

Instead of relying on gut instinct or last-minute creative pivots, brands can plan ahead using validated behavioral benchmarks without the need for artificially recreating seasonal conditions. The result? More confident creative decisions, stronger seasonal performance, and packaging that's built to deliver no matter how short the shelf window.

VALIDATE SHELF PERFORMANCE WITH PACKFLASH

With clear direction with help from unPACKED and refined designs from Pack.AI, Marisol still has one question left to answer: Will this pack work at shelf?

As a small brand without a strong retail foothold, she can't afford to miss. Her packaging doesn't just need to look good in isolation; it needs to perform in the real world, surrounded by competitors, distractions, and merchandising quirks that were beyond her control. And, while her team values AI-driven research, leveraging primary shopper data, they also want to ensure the packaging is put in front of actual shoppers, too.

PackFlash allowed Marisol to test her new packaging in simulated retail environments, revealing how well the design would perform when placed in front of shoppers. It measured shelf behavior, including what shoppers noticed, how easily they found products, what they understood, and most importantly whether they'd choose it.

This step wasn't optional. For a brand manager like Marisol, PackFlash offered the confidence to move forward knowing that her packaging worked in practice. And if something didn't land? She had the behavioral diagnostics to fix it fast.

She wasn't guessing. She was validating.

With PackFlash, Marisol can now walk into buyer meetings or pitch to new retailers with data showing that her brand stands out, communicates clearly, and converts interest into purchase even without big-budget shelf placement or national awareness.

For a small brand in a high-stakes environment, that kind of validation doesn't just level the playing field. It changes the game.

EXPANDING REACH WITH PRECISION AND CONFIDENCE

Reaching new and niche audiences isn't easy, especially for emerging brands like Marisol's. She's not just trying to stand out. She's trying to do it in an environment that's crowded, fragmented, and constantly shifting.

Between digital shelves and physical aisles, different merchandising systems, inconsistent placements, and a sea of similar-looking products, the retail landscape has never been more complex. For a small brand with limited visibility and budget, it's an uphill battle. Every design choice has to work harder to attract attention, communicate benefits, and reinforce credibility in a split second.

What changes everything is the ability to test early, iterate quickly, and understand exactly how packaging performs across shelf formats and consumer mindsets. Instead of taking a shot in the dark on what will resonate or relying on trial and error, Marisol can now approach her design process with clarity and precision. She can identify what shoppers notice, what cues they associate with quality or wellness, and how her brand compares to others in the category. She can adjust before launch, not after.

This shift allows smaller brands to move with the confidence of larger ones and to make faster decisions without sacrificing accuracy. In Marisol's case, it means she's no longer sidelined by shelf complexity or limited in what she can research. She can show up in the right channels, speak to the right audiences, and compete more effectively regardless of size or spend.

But while Marisol's challenges are rooted in retail conditions, other brands face a different kind of complexity: business alignment. We'll next turn our focus to Steven, a global brand leader navigating a redesign across international markets. In the next chapter, we shift from visibility to alignment, from helping a small brand get noticed to helping a global brand reach consensus.

Because at scale, the hardest part isn't always the shopper. It's the system.

TL;DR: Level the Playing Field

- Challenge: Small and emerging brands like Marisol's face an uphill battle in crowded, chaotic retail environments. With limited shelf space, constrained budgets, and fierce competition from larger players, standing out, getting chosen, and converting shoppers is harder than ever.
- Traditional Limitations: New brands often lack access to timely, affordable, and actionable insights. Research has historically been expensive, slow, and inaccessible, especially when testing early-stage ideas, niche audiences, or seasonal variants. Without behavioral benchmarks or predictive products, brands were left guessing what might work.
- Our Solution: We give smaller brands big-brand power by combining unPACKED, Pack.AI, PackFlash, and PPS. These products enable faster testing, smarter iteration, and confident decision-making grounded in real shopper behavior. Brands like Marisol's can diagnose barriers, benchmark visibility, explore creative options, and validate pack performance. All within tight timelines and budgets.
  - Key Benefits:
    - unPACKED helps identify category norms, white space, and visibility benchmarks.
    - Pack.AI enables rapid early-stage testing of dozens of design routes with real behavioral KPIs.
    - PackFlash provides shelf-context validation with actual shoppers to confirm performance.
    - PPS delivers a clear, quantified prediction of sales impact to guide final design decisions.
    - Seasonal variants and niche audiences can be tested and modeled without costly fieldwork.

- Impact: Soupergirl used Pack.AI, PackFlash, and PPS to optimize design and lift sales. Marisol overcame visibility barriers and shelf competition to refine her design with data-backed clarity. Kleenex proved how subtle seasonal packaging can drive repeat purchases. These examples show that with the right products, small brands or seasonal products don't just compete, they win.

Chapter 9.

THE IMPORTANCE OF BUSINESS ALIGNMENT

Ben & Jerry's embarked on a global packaging refresh, one that needed to modernize their design while preserving the brand's iconic identity. The goal wasn't to reinvent the wheel but to evolve it: strengthen appetite appeal, reinforce distinctive brand assets, and ensure the new design resonated across diverse international markets. With both dairy and nondairy lines in play, Ben & Jerry's faced a multilayered task: optimize the design for performance, consistency, and cultural relevance around the world. To deliver the clarity and confidence Ben & Jerry's needed, our team deployed a 3-phase research program:

- Pack.AI to screen early-stage design routes and quickly identify a lead contender based on behavioral performance data
- Qualitative research to explore refinements across both dairy and nondairy formats, revealing how design elements impacted shopper understanding and emotional connection
- PackFlash to validate the final designs in 5 key global markets through quantitative behavioral testing in real shelf environments

This combination of predictive modeling, qualitative depth, and behavioral validation gave the team a complete picture of how the new design would perform functionally, emotionally, and commercially across regions.

Across the research phases, Ben & Jerry's gained strong indicators that the refreshed design would improve performance. The new visual system lifted appetite appeal, reinforced core brand assets, and improved communication consistency, which was particularly important for emerging markets where brand familiarity wasn't guaranteed. Each round of research informed the next, leading to a unified, insight-driven final direction.

The new packaging rolled out successfully across international markets. Teams walked away not only with a stronger design but also with clear proof of its effectiveness backed by behavioral data, cross-market insights, and shopper response. The refresh wasn't just a cosmetic update. It was a strategic win rooted in the kind of research that brings alignment, confidence, and commercial results.[42]

THE GLOBAL BUSINESS ALIGNMENT STORM

Earlier, we met Steven, a global brand manager of a major oral care brand tasked with expanding into a new market: Vietnam. His goal is clear: introduce the brand in a way that preserves global consistency while adapting to local expectations. But as soon as the redesign discussions began, he found himself in the middle of a storm.

The insights team holds firm to historical data that suggests the current pack still worked, at least for existing local customers. Marketing wants a bold shift to appeal to global consumers. Design mocks up a minimalist system. Sales doesn't want to rock the boat with retailers. And the CEO, feeling the pressure of quarterly earnings, just wants to use what works in the US.

What Steven quickly realizes is that he isn't just leading a redesign. He is navigating a deep misalignment of priorities, incentives, and mental models. Each team has its own idea of what "good" looks like. Each brings valid points to the table.

But without a shared framework or common reference point, the conversation keeps circling. Strategy becomes stalled by subjectivity. Packaging decisions should be a catalyst for growth. Instead, they become a game of tug-of-war.

What Steven needs isn't just a new design. He needs alignment: a way to unify perspectives, ground opinions in behavioral data, and ensure that decisions made in one meeting won't get reversed in the next.

This kind of cross-functional alignment is one of the most underestimated challenges in packaging research today. Even the best insights are meaningless if they can't be understood, communicated, and acted on by everyone in the room. Our predictive and diagnostic products help turn packaging research into a shared language that gets marketing, design, insights, *and* leadership moving in the same direction. For Steven (and so many teams like his), alignment isn't just a process fix. It's a strategic unlock.

THE BUSINESS ALIGNMENT PROBLEM

Alignment isn't glamorous, but it's essential. In packaging research, the biggest breakthroughs are often less about discovering the perfect design and more about getting everyone to agree on what success looks like. And that's where things start to fall apart.

The reality is, most packaging decisions involve multiple stakeholders, each with their own priorities, KPIs, and ways of interpreting research. Insights teams focus on data rigor and methodological soundness. Designers want creative latitude and visual innovation. Marketers are under pressure to launch fast, tell a compelling brand story, and make the packaging pop. And executives? They want decision precision and confidence. Not ambiguity. Not trade-offs. Just a clear, data-backed recommendation they can rally behind.

That's the tension: different departments speaking entirely different languages. Often, a research report is built around the metrics insights agreed to track, only to land in the hands of sales or marketing, who are focused on entirely different questions. What felt aligned at commissioning gets lost in translation. The result? A 40-page report filled with statistical jargon or inconclusive results, which stalls the project. The report gets picked apart, reinterpreted, or simply ignored, because it doesn't meet the needs of everyone at the table. The research wasn't wrong; it wasn't built to be shared across functions.

So, decisions are delayed, and budgets get wasted.

That's why alignment has become one of the biggest modern challenges in packaging development: because the team must agree across functions. Research that delivers a shared narrative everyone can act on provides a common language that turns data into decisions.

This is where we have excelled: predictability and consistency delivered via productized solutions. When everyone is using the same approach, and working from the same behavioral truths, alignment stops being the exception and starts being the norm.

We align people around what matters most at the end of it all: impact on sales.

Alignment issues aren't always about miscommunication; they're often about missing context. Teams might be reading the same report, but they're doing so through completely different lenses. We've seen situations where even a small discrepancy (like the preferred hierarchy of 2 lines of copy) leads to full-blown disagreement. One person reads a bolded claim at the top of a list as most important; another sees it as stealing too much attention from what is directly beneath it. These interpretive differences multiply fast when research lacks behavioral grounding. What's needed isn't just data, it's interpretive alignment: a shared baseline that removes uncertainty and helps every stakeholder, whether it be brand, design, insights, marketing, or sales, see the same thing the same way. That's why we rely so heavily on our 4S framework. It gives everyone an effective and consistent language to select and interpret KPIs and make confident, shared decisions.

COLGATE DAILY BRIGHTNESS: EXPANDING INTO CHINA

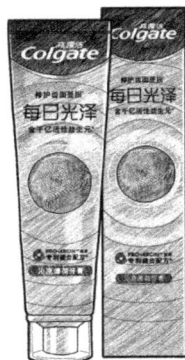

In 2023, Colgate set out to launch Daily Brightness Toothpaste, a new product designed to meet the growing demand for daily oral health solutions in post-pandemic China. But in a crowded category, the stakes were high. The packaging needed to do more than look good—it had to work hard to win trial and clearly communicate the product's point of difference.

That's where we came in. Before launch, Colgate turned to us to evaluate 3 design routes using our flagship PackFlash product. Our goal: identify which design best inspired purchase at shelf while clearly signaling the brand's unique molecular technology benefit.

One design quickly rose to the top. With its gradient color palette, innovative silver-plated cap, and eye-catching 3D "shine ball" visual, it didn't just attract attention, it delivered on clarity and conversion. The chosen pack met our normative trial expectations, giving the team the confidence to move forward with a design that clearly communicated "healthy shine" in an intuitive and engaging way.

This project shows what happens when behavioral science meets bold design. By testing early and validating quickly, Colgate brought a standout pack to market backed by data and built to win.[43]

NAVIGATE GLOBAL-TO-LOCAL EXPANSION

Now, let's get back to Steven. His challenge isn't just designing a successful Vietnam pack. It's aligning cross-functional teams (marketing, design, sales, R&D) across regions, each with their own priorities, to agree on a cohesive, effective packaging strategy.

He can solve for this challenge by analyzing a category-level report for his brand, and he can do it specifically in Vietnam. Using a customized *unPACKED: Oral Care Report*, Steven can learn:

1. Regional Diagnostics and Comparisons: To move forward with confidence, Steven needs to understand how the category behaves in each region. He reviews category-level reports from key markets to compare visual trends, shopper behavior, and brand clustering. These comparisons help him identify:
   A. Visual strategies that consistently lead to strong performance
   B. Market-specific nuances that affect pack design and messaging
   C. Tactics that could unify the brand globally or differentiate it locally

2. Shelf Reality and Strategic Design Inputs: By understanding what packaging elements are driving visibility and choice in the Vietnam market, Steven can assess whether a contrast-based approach (standing out from local players) or a more conforming strategy makes sense. He can also uncover how major brands are displayed at shelf, which attributes they're emphasizing, and what shopper needs may still be unmet.

3. Actionable Design Briefs Across Regions: These insights inform the creative strategy. Steven works with his team to define what must stay consistent across markets (such as brand equities or logo architecture) and what can flex locally (such as color palettes, structures, or callouts). This allows design teams to work from a shared brief rooted in behavioral data, not subjective preferences.

4. Clarity That Drives Consensus: With concrete, observed shopper insights in hand, Steven brings stakeholders into alignment. Internal teams no longer argue from opinion; they align on facts. Discussions shift from "what might work" to "what works," and Steven can guide the team toward a pack design that preserves the brand's global integrity while meeting regional needs.

Predictive diagnostics at the regional category level gives Steven the confidence to move forward with a pack that performs in Vietnam without compromising the brand's global identity.

BUILDING CONSENSUS WITH BEHAVIORAL TESTING

After using category-level diagnostics to understand the shelf dynamics in Vietnam, Steven has a much clearer view of how the market behaves and where his brand can play. But insight alone isn't enough. He still needs to bring his teams along with him.

With multiple functions and regions weighing in, aligning on a final design requires more than a strategic foundation; it requires shared evidence. That's where early-stage performance testing with Pack.AI becomes essential. By evaluating how different pack designs perform with real consumers, Steven can keep teams grounded in the same behavioral KPIs and move from strategic theory to confident action.

CREATE A SHARED LANGUAGE ACROSS TEAMS

Our predictive model turns early-stage creative ideas into performance data. For Steven, this means every stakeholder, whether in marketing, sales, insights, or design, can view and compare packaging options using the same set of behavioral KPIs: visibility, shoppability, appeal, and purchase. Rather than debating aesthetics or personal preferences, the team can align around how designs perform in front of shoppers. It becomes a conversation about outcomes and sales impact, not opinions.

COMPARE GLOBAL VERSUS LOCAL DESIGNS AT SCALE

Steven can upload a range of design options, some rooted in global brand equity and others tailored for Vietnam's market, and see how they perform with local audiences. He doesn't need to guess which elements to preserve or adapt. He can test dozens of combinations, isolate the strongest performers, and identify which changes strengthen relevance without compromising brand recognition.

FACILITATE FASTER DECISION-MAKING
ACROSS MARKETS

Instead of waiting weeks to test a handful of designs, Steven can run rapid, iterative tests across a broad range of concepts. This allows regional teams to bring forward localized ideas while still staying connected to global guidelines. With every round of testing, Steven refines alignment, bringing creative exploration and commercial strategy into sync.

With global and regional teams now working from the same set of behavioral metrics, Steven moves closer to packaging that balances consistency with local relevance.

But alignment on direction isn't the same as making the final call. As he narrows the field to a few top contenders, Steven needs one last layer of confidence: a clear, predictive signal of which design will drive sales.

PACKFLASH: A CROSS-FUNCTIONAL REALITY CHECK

Steven doesn't just need new packaging—he needs alignment. Every team brings a different vision for what the pack should do, and every stakeholder has a stake in the outcome. But none of them can agree on which direction is right—or even what "right" looks like.

This is where PackFlash becomes invaluable.

Instead of debating opinions in the boardroom, Steven uses PackFlash to simulate real-world shopper behavior across multiple international markets. By testing each design direction in a controlled, behavioral environment, he generates hard data on what shoppers see, understand, and choose.

And it delivers:

- Neutral, behavior-based evidence that cuts through subjective bias
- Clear visibility into which design performs best across key behavioral KPIs like findability, differentiation, and purchase
- Market-specific diagnostics that help reconcile global consistency with local nuance
- A basis for productive cross-functional conversation: Everyone sees the same results, and debate shifts from "what looks better" to "what works better"

For Steven, PackFlash isn't just a testing tool; it's a consensus accelerator.

As a final step, Steven uses PPS to bring clarity and confidence to the final stage of his redesign process. After working through upstream diagnostics and iterative testing, he's left with a handful of strong contenders, but stakeholders are still divided. By distilling complex behavioral data into a single, predictive score calibrated against real-world sales outcomes, PPS gives Steven's team a shared signal they can rally around.

Ultimately, it becomes the decision accelerator Steven needs. It transforms research from a conversation starter into a decision *closer*, ensuring the chosen design looks great and performs where it counts most: in market.

This approach gives him the behavioral evidence he needs to align the C-suite, gain support from the insights team, reassure the sales team, and bring clarity to a decision that had stalled for weeks.

The result? A validated design direction, stakeholder alignment, and momentum without compromise.

KEEBLER: BALANCING HERITAGE WITH GROWTH UNDER NEW OWNERSHIP

When Ferrero acquired Keebler, they set out to modernize the brand without losing what made it beloved. Their goal was to extend a fresh redesign across key product lines including Fudge Stripes, Chips Deluxe, E. L. Fudge, and Sandies to drive incremental sales. But with an established identity deeply ingrained in shoppers' minds, the new ownership faced a critical challenge: how to align innovation with brand equity, keeping both new executives and loyal consumers on board.

To navigate this strategic transition, Ferrero partnered with us to evaluate new design directions using PackFlash. The tool provided deep insight into how each proposed pack performed on critical behavioral KPIs, specifically visibility, shoppability, purchase intent, and taste appeal, while ensuring the essence of the Keebler brand wasn't lost in translation.

The result was a winning pack that outperformed expectations across all key metrics. With slight adjustments to brand name placement, character usage, and food imagery, Ferrero successfully created a design that felt fresh without alienating established shoppers. The redesign not only aligned internal stakeholders across the old and new guard, but it also resonated strongly with consumers, setting the stage for renewed growth.

This project shows the power of packaging to bridge organizational change. When ownership shifts, packaging research can become a unifying tool, helping diverse teams align on what matters most: visibility, clarity, and relevance at shelf.[44]

WHY ALIGNMENT IS A BUSINESS IMPERATIVE

Without alignment, even the most well-researched packaging initiative can stall or, worse, fall apart. Teams waste cycles debating direction. Research gets buried in decks no one reads. Creative decisions are delayed, reversed, or diluted. And promising ideas? They never make it to shelf.

But with alignment, the entire process transforms. Decisions get made faster. Teams collaborate with more clarity. Creative energy flows with purpose. And most importantly, the packaging not only looks better—it performs better, too.

Steven's team now operates with that clarity. They're not fighting over opinions; they're anchored in shared products, shared data, and a common definition of success. The insights team sees what the designers see. Marketing speaks the same language as sales. Everyone is looking at the same evidence and drawing from the same source of truth.

That's an added value of our products. Not just the quality of the research itself, but how that research becomes usable, repeatable, and shared across an entire organization. They aren't just predictive and diagnostic products. They're alignment engines, giving teams the clarity and cohesion they need to move forward with confidence, together.

The alignment Steven achieved isn't just about smoother meetings or faster approvals. It represents something deeper: a shift in how organizations make decisions grounded in behavior, evidence, and, importantly, shared understanding.

That's what this book has been building toward. Not just smarter products or better packaging, but a new standard for how we approach the intersection of brands and behavior. Our model is about providing more time for insights and measuring what matters: sales.

In the final chapter, we'll share our Plan Forward, a distillation of everything we believe about the future of packaging, shopper insights, and decision-making in a complex, fast-moving world. It's not just a summary. It's a stake in the ground.

TL;DR: The Importance of Business Alignment

- Challenge: Packaging decisions often stall due to cross-functional misalignment. Each team brings different priorities and interpretations to the table, making it difficult to reach consensus on what "success" looks like.
- Traditional Limitation: Research is frequently siloed, built for one department's lens but irrelevant or misaligned for others. As a result, insights are ignored, creative direction gets stalled, and packaging decisions are delayed or reversed.
- Our Solution: Our suite of predictive and diagnostic products—unPACKED, Pack.AI, PackFlash, and PPS—turns packaging research into a shared language that drives faster, more confident, and more collaborative decision-making across teams.
  - Key Benefits:
    - unPACKED gives regional and global teams behavioral benchmarks and category insights to align on creative strategy across markets.
    - Pack.AI enables early-stage testing of design routes using shared behavioral KPIs that every team can interpret and act on.
    - PackFlash validates final contenders in real shelf environments, providing neutral, behavior-based evidence that unites stakeholders around what works.
    - PPS delivers a single predictive benchmark tied to real-world sales impact, offering the clarity needed to finalize decisions with confidence.
    - The entire system provides a shared decision framework across functions, reducing debate and accelerating progress toward high-performing packaging.

- Impact: Ben & Jerry's used a combination of Pack.AI, qualitative research, and PackFlash to create a global packaging refresh rooted in behavioral data. Colgate aligned multiple teams around a new launch in China with PackFlash insights. Ferrero's redesign of Keebler brought together legacy and new leadership by using behavioral testing to preserve equity while driving growth. Steven used our full suite to align global and local teams on a Vietnam redesign, transforming stakeholder conflict into strategic momentum.

Chapter 10.

THE PLAN FORWARD

This chapter isn't a recap. We're not here to rehash what's already been said, and we're not going to give you a checklist of everything we've covered.

This is something different. A perspective shift.

We're closing the book with a clear point of view: a manifesto for a new era of packaging decisions. One that moves faster, aligns smarter, and stays grounded in what shoppers do. It's a shift from silos to shared understanding.

It's a POV we and our team members share: We *strongly* believe in Behaviorally's manifesto and what it stands for.

If you take one thing from this chapter, let it be this: The future of packaging belongs to brands that can act quickly, align completely, and make decisions based on evidence—not on opinion.

This is our call to action. Embrace behavioral insight. Build smarter systems. Let's move forward together, and with purpose.

A NEW ERA FOR PACKAGING DECISIONS

The established frameworks of packaging research served their purpose, but they are no longer sufficient for the demands of today's market. Models once defined by lengthy timelines, siloed execution, and retrospective insights can no longer deliver the speed, precision, or alignment required to compete.

Packaging is more than a creative expression; it is a strategic business asset. It must capture attention and convert it into action within moments, whether on a crowded store shelf or a digital interface. And with the right infrastructure, brands can now understand, before launching, what will drive measurable results.

This is the shift: from research as a retrospective output to insight as a forward-looking performance system. The brands that lead in this next era will be those that operationalize 3 critical capabilities:

1. First-party behavioral data that captures real shopper decisions
2. Sales calibration that links behavioral signals to in-market outcomes
3. Predictive products that transform insight into scalable, confident action

The new era is about organizational clarity, commercial precision, and enterprise-wide alignment around what works.

We possess the data, the models, and the methodologies. The question is no longer whether we *can* predict packaging performance; it is whether we will build the systems and culture to act decisively on those predictions.

Let us move forward together, grounded in insight, aligned in purpose, and equipped for outcomes that matter.

THE ENGINE WE'VE BUILT

We've built something disruptive: a predictive engine that turns packaging decisions into performance outcomes. At the core is a system that productizes first-party behavioral data rigorously collected, uniquely structured, and validated over decades. That data is now married to real sales outcomes. AI and machine learning help us scale this engine, but the foundation is behavioral: what real people do, in real contexts, with real impact.

This is not a theoretical model. It's a working system that takes client questions like "Will this design drive sales?" and gives reliable, *repeatable* answers. Ones that reflect real-world outcomes, not just research assumptions. Our data and its structure results in the most powerful packaging prediction platform in the industry.

WHAT WE BELIEVE

This isn't just a methodology. It's a mindset. A new operating system for packaging decisions, built on behavioral science and powered by predictive products. These are the principles that guide us and the principles we believe should guide you, too.

1. **You should never again waste time and budget on a design that doesn't impact the bottom line.** Our predictive engine exists to remove risk. It gives us clarity before the stakes are high. There's no reason to launch blind and waste half of your marketing budget. Use the products. Trust the data.

2. **Packaging research should be a shared language.** When research speaks only to the insights team, it fails. The best products bring everyone to the table, including marketers, designers, analysts, and executives, all aligned around the same evidence. That alignment isn't a luxury; it's what enables speed, precision, and confident decision-making across the

business. Shared insight fuels better collaboration, and better outcomes.

3. **Human creativity and data aren't opposites; they're partners.** Data doesn't kill brave ideas. It makes them smarter. Design boldly, then test, refine, and elevate. When behavior guides creativity, everyone wins.

4. **Behavioral observation beats claimed intent. Every time.** Consumers don't always say what they mean or mean what they say. But their actions speak loudly and clearly. Watch what they do. Build from there.

5. **The shelf is one of your most valuable marketing spaces.** Whether in store or online, it's where choices are made and brands are built. Treat your packaging like the media channel it is. Optimize it and expect it to provide high performance impact like any other critical marketing piece in the mix.

These are more than beliefs. They're imperatives for anyone serious about maximizing in today's market. The brands that succeed won't be the ones that guess right. They'll be the ones that build systems for learning, aligning, and acting at speed.

While our predictive engine has transformed how consumer goods brands make packaging decisions, the same principles apply across the entire marketing mix. Leading with pack is a smart starting point—it's visible, impactful, and measurable, but it's only the beginning. When brands adopt behavioral science, productization, and predictive models as a system, they gain a competitive advantage across advertising, media, shopper marketing, and innovation. The future is about building an integrated, insights-driven engine that drives performance everywhere.

Lead with pack, but don't stop there.

FROM PROJECTS TO IMPACT: A BOOM IN WHAT COMES NEXT

Our engine changes the role of insight itself. People are no longer stuck "doing" research; they're free to use it. To advise, to interpret, to guide. Insight becomes a copilot, not a passenger; we report and influence. Humans doing what only humans can do.

As predictive output becomes more automated, the human value expands toward impact and helps clients understand what the data says and what to do next.

More predictions unlock more possibilities. The more clients rely on predictive packaging products, the more space we create for giving advice on design and creative development. Increased confidence in prediction creates demand for smart complements. Think qualitative explorations, deeper diagnostics, stronger storytelling, and faster iteration.

That's where predictions go next.

THE ROAD AHEAD

Behavioral science is the foundation of how we understand shoppers today. Predictive AI is no longer a futuristic concept or a nice-to-have; it's essential infrastructure for fast, confident decision-making. And packaging research? It has to evolve. From static, point-in-time reports tied to a moment, to strategic products that shape decisions in real time.

We're not just inviting you to use new products. We're inviting you to rethink what packaging research can do. To move it out of the testing silo and into the heart of everyday brand strategy. To bring it into the rooms where decisions are made as you need them and when it's relevant. Become the person in your organization who speaks behavioral fluency. Who champions clarity over complexity. Who doesn't just ask for better data but knows how to act on it. Because the next era of packaging is about better research and better leadership.

And while we're starting with packaging, we're not stopping there. If this is what's possible in packaging, what might be possible elsewhere?

This predictive engine can scale. Imagine applying it across different areas of the marketing mix including creative, media, innovation. Anywhere decisions hinge on what people will do, not just on what they say. That's where we're headed: toward a broader application of behavioral prediction, because it's a system that can exist anywhere we can get our hands on behavioral, first-party data.

A CALL FOR HIGHER STANDARDS

The predictive engine is built, and it delivers. The imperative now lies with the industry: to elevate expectations of what packaging research should achieve. It is no longer sufficient to assume packaging will contribute to growth. Stakeholders must require that it demonstrably does.

For brand leaders, marketers, and insights professionals, this is a defining opportunity. Demand that your packaging investments deliver measurable return. Insist on predictive clarity, not just directional guidance. Expect that design decisions, like any other strategic lever, be grounded in evidence, not assumption.

This is not a call to conduct more research. It is a call to build systems that support faster, smarter, and more accountable decision-making. In a marketplace that rewards precision and agility, the brands that succeed will be those who embrace this shift first, who move beyond measurement to true performance management.

And while this book focused on packaging, the principles

apply far beyond the pack. Behavioral clarity, predictive infrastructure, and enterprise alignment are not just packaging imperatives: They're the future of insights, innovation, and marketing at large. Packaging is where we've built the engine. But it's just the beginning.

The future belongs to the bold. Lead the pack.

ACKNOWLEDGMENTS

This book would not have been possible without the partnership, insight, and trust of our clients. We're fortunate to work with some of the world's most thoughtful and innovative consumer goods brands: teams who don't just embrace behavioral science but push us to apply it in new and meaningful ways. Your challenges inspire our best thinking, and your openness made this book stronger.

A special thanks to those who contributed directly, offering their stories, experiences, and perspectives including Bianca Pryor, Liz Riley Raukohl, Abhishek Deb, Lori Herman, and Urszula Paliwoda.

To our colleagues at Behaviorally, past and present: Thank you for being all in. This book reflects the work we've done together: the ideas we've tested, the products we've built, and the future we're shaping. We're proud to work alongside a team so committed to client success, grounded in science, and energized by innovation. Your belief in the vision behind this book was felt on every page.

To Janice Lai: Thank you for your tireless coordination, sharp attention to detail, and ability to keep all the moving parts in sync. You've been instrumental at every step.

To Thibault Cousot: Thank you for your technical leadership and guidance on AI concepts, which brought clarity and depth to our story.

To Brendan Cox: Thank you for your support with the database and predictive modeling insights that helped ground our work in real-world credibility.

To Sheryl Brie: Thank you for your expertise in heuristics and behavioral science. Your contributions strengthened our examples.

To Elliot Young, founder of Perception Research Services, and Scott Young: Thank you for your foundational influence on the industry and for allowing us to quote you in this book.

Finally, to our publishing team at Lioncrest, Jamie, Lisa, and everyone behind the scenes: We thank you for your partnership, editorial insight, and dedication to getting this book into the world with clarity and purpose.

ABOUT THE AUTHORS

ALEX HUNT

Alex Hunt is a global leader in the data and insights industry with a passion for applying behavioral science and technology to solve one of the most critical challenges in marketing: predicting human behavior. With over 2 decades of experience guiding data-driven growth, Alex has helped some of the world's most iconic brands unlock the power of consumer insight to understand the market and shape it.

As CEO of Behaviorally, Alex has led the company's strategic transformation into a provider of predictive digital products focused on helping brands win the most important moment in marketing: the purchase transaction. Under his leadership, Behaviorally has become a pioneer in leveraging first-party behavioral data and predictive analytics to help brands optimize their packaging and retail presence.

In 2025, Alex was elected to the Insights Association's Board of Directors, a recognition of his ongoing commitment to advancing the data, insights, and analytics profession. In this role, he collaborates with fellow industry leaders to shape long-term strategies and standards, promote engagement across the insights community, and advocate for innovation that reflects the rapidly evolving needs of the marketplace.

A frequent speaker at global conferences and industry events, Alex is a strong advocate for turning insight into impact. He believes behavioral data is only as valuable as the systems built to scale it, and that real progress comes when organizations stop treating research as a retrospective report and start treating it as a performance engine.

A native of the United Kingdom, Alex now lives in Connecticut with his wife, Pam, and daughter, Gabriella. Outside of work, he enjoys spending time with his family.

At his core, Alex is driven by one question: How do we better predict what people will do? This book is part of his answer: a manifesto for a more predictive, commercially grounded future for packaging research and beyond.

MATT SALEM

Matt Salem has spent over 2 decades at the intersection of behavioral insight and marketing strategy, helping the world's leading brands decode how packaging drives shopper decisions and, ultimately, sales. As SVP of Customer Success at Behaviorally, Matt brings deep expertise across packaging, merchandising, and the path to purchase, along with a passion for turning complex data into clear, actionable narratives.

A trusted advisor to global clients and a dynamic presence at industry events, he is known for his ability to make insight approachable. Whether he's on stage, leading a strategy session, or hosting a guest on Behaviorally's *Our Best Behavior* podcast, Matt brings energy, clarity, and a genuine curiosity to every conversation.

Originally from New York and now based in North Jersey, Matt balances his professional passion for precision with a personal love of the outdoors, fitness, craft beer, and cigars. Most importantly, he's a proud father to Niessen and Nyla, who are a constant source of inspiration.

Matt believes great research tells an insightful, easy-to-understand story—and that great packaging is always consumer-led. That belief has shaped his career, his perspective, and now, this book.

NOTES

1   Behaviorally, "Chocolates unPACKED USA Report," internal presentation PDF, September 2024. Provided by Behaviorally.

2   Behaviorally, "Chocolates unPACKED USA Report."

3   Grand View Research, "Chocolate Market Size, Share & Trends Analysis Report By Product (Traditional, Artificial), By Distribution Channel (Supermarket & Hypermarket, Convenience Store, Online), By Region, And Segment Forecasts, 2024–2030," January 2024, https://www.grandviewresearch.com/industry-analysis/chocolate-market; Emergen Research, "Chocolate Market Size Worth USD 161.99 Billion in 2032," *Yahoo Finance*, accessed June 3, 2025, https://finance.yahoo.com/news/chocolate-market-size-worth-usd-191300029.html.

4   International Cocoa Organization, "Chocolate Industry," *International Cocoa Organization*, accessed February 14, 2025, https://www.icco.org/chocolate-industry/.

5   "Our Promise," Tony's Chocolonely, accessed May 7, 2025, https://www.tonyschocolonely.com/us/en/our-mission.

6   Tony's Chocolonely, *Annual FAIR Report 2023/2024* (Tony's Chocolonely, 2024, accessed May 26, 2025), https://online.flippingbook.com/view/189607595/.

7   Judy Rice, "New Design, and a 40% Sales Boost, for Gentleman Jack," *Packaging World*, April 8, 2010, https://www.packworld.com/leaders-new/materials/containers/article/13347714/new-design-and-a-40-sales-boost-for-gentleman-jack.

8   "Consumer Packaged Goods (CPG) Market Size Forecast 2034," Towards Packaging, accessed May 7, 2025, https://www.towardspackaging.com/insights/consumer-packaged-goods-cpg-market-sizing.

9   Consumer Brands Association, "CPG Industry Drives US Economy with $2.5 Trillion Contribution and 22.3 Million Jobs," news release, October 22, 2024, https://consumerbrandsassociation.org/press-releases/cpg-industry-drives-u-s-economy-with-2-5-trillion-contribution-and-22-3-million-jobs/.

10 GOOD Staff, "Researchers Tested a Bottle of Fiji Water Against a Glass of Tap Water and Here's What They Found," GOOD, February 11, 2025, https://www.good.is/researchers-tested-a-bottle-of-fiji-water-against-a-glass-of-tap-water-and-heres-what-they-found-ex2.

11 Julie Pennell, "Do You Know This Simple Trick to Get Ketchup out of Glass Heinz Bottles?," Today, October 26, 2017, https://www.today.com/food/how-get-ketchup-out-bottle-trick-heinz-57-t118061.

12 Julie Pennell, "Do You Know...Glass Heinz Bottles?"

13 "Solving the Ketchup Ooze Problem," CBS News, April 3, 2000, https://www.cbsnews.com/news/solving-the-ketchup-ooze-problem/; and Martin Lindstrom, "Here for Heinz: Why the Glass Bottle Still Rules the Brand," LinkedIn, May 25, 2017, https://www.linkedin.com/pulse/here-heinz-why-glass-bottle-still-rules-brand-martin-lindstrom/.

14 Bennie Valencia, "Why Packaging Redesign Matters: Heinz, Justin's, and RXBar Before-and-After Success Stories," Incrementum Digital, July 22, 2024, https://incrementumdigital.com/blog/retail-media/packaging-redesign-audit-heinz-justins-rxbar-success-stories/.

15 Taylor Huang, "RXBar's Old Packaging Is Totally Unrecognizable," Mashed, February 5, 2023, https://www.mashed.com/1187121/rxbars-old-packaging-is-totally-unrecognizable/.

16 Megan Bruneau, "$600M Exit: How RXBAR's Dyslexic Founder Outsmarted the Protein Industry," Forbes, May 22, 2025, https://www.forbes.com/sites/meganbruneau/2025/05/22/special-education-to-600m-exit-how-rxbars-dyslexic-founder-outsmarted-the-protein-industry/.

17 Natalie Zmuda, "Tropicana Line's Sales Plunge 20% Post-Rebranding," Ad Age, April 2, 2009, https://adage.com/article/news/tropicana-line-s-sales-plunge-20-post-rebranding/135735/; Neurensics, "How Tropicana Lost $30 Million Due to New Packaging," Neurensics, accessed June 3, 2025, https://www.neurensics.com/en/packaging-learning-4-how-tropicana-lost-30-million-dollars-due-to-new-packaging; Marion Andrivet, "What to Learn from Tropicana's Packaging Redesign Failure?," The Branding Journal, May 1, 2015, https://www.thebrandingjournal.com/2015/05/what-to-learn-from-tropicanas-packaging-redesign-failure/.

18 Anne Marie Mohan, "Celestial's Package Refresh 'Reflects the Goodness Inside,'" Packaging World, November 3, 2015, https://www.packworld.com/leaders-new/materials/cartons-boxes/article/13369004/celestials-package-refresh-reflects-the-goodness-inside.

19 Jenna Blumenfeld, "How Celestial Seasonings Strengthened Consumer Trust Through Packaging," New Hope Network, October 19, 2016, https://www.newhope.com/brands/how-celestial-seasonings-strengthened-consumer-trust-through-packaging.

20 David Salazar, "Celestial Seasonings Intros 5 New Flavors, Brings Back Classic Packaging," *Drug Store News*, September 15, 2016, https://drugstorenews.com/center-store/celestial-seasonings-intros-new-flavors-brings-back-classic-packaging.

21 Nestlé, "Nestlé Introduces Vital Pursuit Brand to Support GLP-1 Users and Consumers Focused on Weight Loss and Management," news release, May 21, 2024, https://www.nestleusa.com/media/pressreleases/vital-pursuit-glp-1-weight-manage.

22 Behaviorally, "Nestlé Vital Pursuit Case Study," internal presentation PDF, 2024. Provided by Behaviorally.

23 Behaviorally, "Ritz Toasted Chips Case Study," internal presentation PDF, 2025. Provided by Behaviorally.

24 Theresa Christine Johnson, "How One Brand's New Design Revived an Entire Category," *DIELINE*, January 22, 2018, https://thedieline.com/how-one-brands-new-design-revived-an-entire-category/.

25 Patty Odell, "Lean Cuisine's Package Redesign Drives $58 Million Sales Increase in One Year," *Chief Marketer*, May 4, 2017, https://chiefmarketer.com/lean-cuisines-package-redesign-drives-58-million-sales-increase-in-one-year/.

26 Odell, Patty, "Lean Cuisine's Package...Increase in One Year."

27 "Lean Cuisine® Encourages Women to Weigh What Matters," *Nestlé USA*, January 13, 2016, https://www.nestleusa.com/media/pressreleases/lean-cuisine-weigh-this-diet-filter.

28 Daniel Kahneman, *Thinking, Fast and Slow* (Farrar, Straus and Giroux, 2011).

29 Behaviorally, "Nature's Way Case Study," internal presentation PDF, 2025. Provided by Behaviorally.

30 B. J. Fogg, *Tiny Habits: The Small Changes That Change Everything* (Houghton Mifflin Harcourt, 2020).

31 Roger Dooley, *Brainfluence: 100 Ways to Persuade and Convince Consumers with Neuromarketing* (John Wiley & Sons, 2011).

32 Behaviorally, "Chobani Fit Case Study," internal presentation PDF, 2025. Provided by Behaviorally.

33 Behaviorally, "O Organics Case Study," internal presentation PDF, 2025. Provided by Behaviorally.

34 Behaviorally, "Colgate Total Plaque Case Study," internal presentation, 2023. Provided by Behaviorally.

35 Behaviorally, "Pitmaster LT's Case Study," internal presentation PDF, 2024. Provided by Behaviorally.

36 Behaviorally, "Mars Wrigley Extra Case Study," internal presentation PDF, 2025. Provided by Behaviorally.

37 Brooke Kato, "Capri Sun Faces Backlash over Controversial Packaging Change: 'One of the Most Shocking Product Changes in History,'" August 30, 2024, *New York Post*, https://nypost.com/2024/08/30/lifestyle/capri-sun-faces-backlash-over-controversial-packaging-change/; and Grace Snelling, "You Can Now Drink Capri Sun out of a Boring Bottle," *Fast Company*, February 4, 2025, https://www.fastcompany.com/91272333/capri-sun-new-bottle.

38 Behaviorally, "Tom's of Maine," internal presentation PDF, 2025. Provided by Behaviorally.

39 Behaviorally, "Soupergirl Case Study—IIEX NA 2025 Presentation," internal presentation PDF, 2025. Provided by Behaviorally.

40 Ben Tobin, "Walmart, Walgreens, CVS Lock Merchandise to Deter Theft, Frustrates Shopper," *Business Insider*, December 29, 2022, https://www.businessinsider.com/walmart-walgreens-cvs-lock-merchandise-to-deter-theft-frustrates-shoppers-2022-12; Alex Bitter and Dominick Reuter, "Locked-Up Merchandise Is Turning Off Shoppers at CVS, Walgreens, and Other Big Drugstores," *Business Insider*, August 11, 2024, https://www.businessinsider.com/locked-up-merchandise-drugstores-annoys-shoppers-cvs-walgreens-rite-aid-2024-8.

41 Thomas Franck, "Private-label Grocery Brands Boomed During Inflation. Prices are Down, but Store-brand Items Keep Going Higher, *CNBC*, September 16, 2024, https://www.cnbc.com/2024/09/16/future-of-supermarket-store-brands-after-end-of-war-on-inflation.html.

42 Behaviorally, "Ben & Jerry's Pint Ice Cream Case Study," internal presentation PDF, 2025. Provided by Behaviorally.

43 Behaviorally, "Colgate Daily Brightness Toothpaste Case Study," internal presentation PDF, 2025. Provided by Behaviorally.

44 Behaviorally, "Keebler Case Study," internal presentation PDF, 2025. Provided by Behaviorally.

www.ingramcontent.com/pod-product-compliance
Lightning Source LLC
Chambersburg PA
CBHW030507210326
41597CB00013B/821